Angela ♡

Your a great
cook! I know you enjoy
experimenting with your microwave
so have fun ♡

Blessings
&
Friendship

Teresa

The
MICROWAVE
Cookbook and Primer

The
MICROWAVE
Cookbook and Primer

Maryann Zepp

Good Books
Intercourse, Pennsylvania 17534

The Microwave Cookbook and Primer
Copyright © 1987 by Good Books, Intercourse, PA 17534
International Standard Book Number (hardcover): 0-934672-43-1
International Standard Book Number (concealed spiral): 0-934672-44-X
Library of Congress Catalog Card Number: 87-80249

Cover photos: by Brian R. Tolbert/brt Photographic Illustrations
Design by Craig Heisey

Table of Contents

Introduction

The 18 Most Asked Questions By Microwave Users

1

What is a microwave?
- It is a form of radiant heat similar to a radio wave.
- It is about the size of a standard pencil.
- It cannot penetrate metal.
- It passes through paper, glass, and plastic.
- It cannot be stored.
- It does not produce a chemical change in food.

2

How do microwaves cook food?
- They are attracted to water, sugar, and fat molecules, causing those molecules to vibrate.
- That vibration creates friction which in turn produces the heat which cooks the food.
- Microwaves create friction on the outside of the food.
- The inside of the food is cooked by the heat being conducted from the outside in.

3

How does the microwave oven work?

- Most microwave ovens are easily installed by plugging them into regular household grounded outlets.
- The ovens used for testing the recipes in this book were 650 to 700 watts.
- An electrical current activates the magnetron tube which produces microwaves. These microwaves are either deflected by a mode stirrer fan or emitted directly onto the food which is turned by a carousel. Microwaves are also deflected off the metal walls of the oven.

4

Are microwave ovens safe to operate?

- **First review your operator's manual!**
- Usually there are three safety locks which must be engaged before the oven will operate.
- There is no documented proof of injury from radiation from a microwave oven. (There are, however, many incidences of cooking injuries from hot fat and boiling water, regardless of the kind of appliance used.)
- Microwaves cannot leak from the oven because the oven is a metal box.
- Microwaves travel in straight lines so they cannot go around angles to escape.
- The U.S. Government has declared microwave ovens to be absolutely safe without reservations.
- Wearers of shielded pacemakers face no danger in operating a microwave oven. If you have any doubts consult your physician.
- It is essential that only microwave-safe equipment be used in a microwave oven. All recipes in this book presume the use of microwave-safe utensils and containers, whether stated specifically or not.

To test for safety, place a glass measure containing ½ cup of water into the microwave oven. Beside it place the container being tested. Turn the oven on High for 1 minute.

If the water is hot at the end of the minute and the container being tested is cool, it can be safely used in a microwave oven. If, however, the container being tested is warm, it has absorbed microwave energy and may in time crack or break as a result.

5

What should you expect from microwave cooking?

- **Speed**—Generally foods will cook in one-fourth the time required by conventional cooking methods. There are many exceptions to this rule which will be discussed throughout the book.
- **Coolness**—Heat is created within the food so your kitchen will remain cool.
- **Economy**—You are using much less energy to cook the foods since the cooking time is shorter. In addition, you are using less electrical wattage than a conventional electric stove uses.
- **Nutrition**—More vitamins and minerals are retained in the food because of its reduced cooking time. Furthermore, one need not add any or much liquid and salt which dissolve many food nutrients.
- **Color**—Foods retain their natural color.
- **Taste**—Foods retain their natural flavors.
- **Convenience**—Food can be cooked in its serving dish. (Dishes that work in the microwave can also be cleaned in the dishwasher.) Many foods are cooked in disposable materials like paper plates, towels, or napkins.

There is no mess while cooking. There is very little cleanup. And many ovens feature programs which allow you to cook meals while you are away from home.

6

What are some variables I should know about?

- **Density**—This is probably the most important of all variables. The thicker and heavier the food, the longer it will take to cook. Density affects a food's cooking time and placement in the oven. For example, arrange chicken pieces so that the thicker ends are to the outside of the dish where they are hit first by the microwaves. When doing broccoli and cauliflower flowerettes together, place the cauliflower along the outer edge because of its higher density.
- **Volume**—The more food you have the longer it will take to cook. If you microwave one potato, all the microwaves concentrate on it. The number of microwaves in an oven remains constant, so if you microwave four potatoes, they share the microwaves and the cooking time is considerably longer.
- **Starting temperature**—Unless otherwise specified, most directions assume the food to be cooked is at room temperature. If the food is colder it will take longer to cook. (For example, frozen green beans take longer to cook than beans at room temperature.)
- **Moisture content**—It takes longer to cook foods with large volumes of water. Both pasta and soups with stock bases require as much time in the microwave as on a conventional stove. They can be cooked in a microwave oven, but that method will not save time.
- **Standing time**—This is as vital to successful microwaving as the actual cooking time. Standing time finishes the cooking process by allowing the heat on the outside of the food to transfer to the middle. This takes place outside the oven (except for cakes) and for certain foods requires the same amount of time as the cooking process. It takes four minutes to microwave a pound of hamburger and another four minutes of standing time to complete the cooking.

7

When should foods be covered?

Most food should be covered when placed in a microwave oven, for two main reasons: to keep the heat and moisture in, and to keep the oven clean.

If the finished product is to be dry, cover it with a paper product. Waxed paper will keep the heat in and allow the steam to escape. Use it when baking a cake. Paper towels or napkins will absorb extra moisture created in the microwave. Use them to wrap baked products, like breads and rolls.

Plastic wrap or glass lids keep in both the moisture and the heat. Use these to cover roasts and most other high protein foods such as eggs. Cover vegetables with plastic or glass to keep in both the moisture and heat, thus producing steam.

Heavy plastic bags work well for frozen vegetables. Never use a metal twist tie because it will start a fire. Products high in sugar, fat, or water will retain too much heat and melt the plastic.

Nylon cooking bags work very well for conventional as well as microwave cooking. They retain the heat and moisture, contain the mess and make a very convenient package for preparing a meal in a bag. Try meals-in-one (a roast and vegetables, for example) or anything covered with sauces.

Because the microwaves hit the corners and any protrusions first, those areas tend to dry out. Aluminum foil can be used to shield areas that may cook too quickly. Use these coverings to protect the corners on square pans or protrusions like wings on poultry.

(Aluminum foil should be folded smoothly to prevent sparking. But it presents no fire hazard like twisties or conventional metal plates.)

8

Do I need to rotate the dishes or stir the food?

Most microwaves have either a mode stirrer fan or a carousel to prevent over-cooking as a result of "hot spots."

The recipes collected here indicate when to stir food, but it is important to understand why it is frequently necessary. Because food cooks from the outside in, scrambled eggs, for example, should be stirred so the uncooked center is moved to the outside.

If it is not possible to stir the food (such as breads or cakes), it may be necessary to rotate the container so that even baking occurs.

9

What cannot be done successfully in a microwave oven?

- Eggs in the shell will explode. But be sure to see the Egg chapter (pages 34–38) for ways you can cook eggs in the microwave.
- Foods in which steam is the leavening—such as angel food and chiffon cakes, souffles, and popovers—will not work. Their short cooking time and lack of a crisp crust prevents them from developing a structure.
- Toasting or crisping—such as is needed for home fried potatoes or French toast—will not occur naturally but can be obtained with some adjustments.
- Deep fat frying is not recommended because of the temperature required, but pan frying is attainable with small amounts of fats.
- Be careful with anything having a high concentration of fat, sugar, or water, since these foods attract microwaves. Consequently they cook faster and their temperatures will rise more quickly. Examples of these foods are corn syrup, honey, and spaghetti sauce.
- Anything encased must be pierced in some way to allow the steam to escape. This includes packages, such as a box or pouch, a natural casing on liver or sausage, skins on baked potatoes or the membrane of an egg.
- Almost any food in a quantity of more than 6 or 8 servings cannot be prepared more quickly in a microwave oven than on a conventional stove or oven. The more food there is to be cooked, the longer the cooking time required to cook it.

10

What are power levels?

The power level refers to the amount of power being emitted from the oven. If you are using a 650 watt oven at full power you will be using 650 watts. If you operate that oven at 50% power you will be using 325 watts. While some microwave ovens refer to percentages, others designate levels from "1" to "10," and still others use gradations from "Low" to "High." If your oven uses a scale from 1 to 10, add a zero to each figure to arrive at the percentage of power. If you have further questions, consult your manual to discover how much power you are using.

11

How do I choose the correct power level?

Use the same judgment as you do when cooking conventionally. The more quickly the food is to be cooked, the higher the power level. For instance, to boil water use "High," but to cook a roast use a lower power level so the meat gets done in the middle without overcooking on the outside.

A "High" (100%) power level is assumed in the recipes in this collection unless otherwise stated.

Power Levels by Percentage in a Microwave Oven	Power Levels in a Microwave Oven	Temperatures in a Conventional Oven
10% Warm	1	100°F
20% Low	2	150°F
30% Defrost	3	200°F
40% Med-Low	4	250°F
50% Medium	5	300°F
60% Bake	6	350°F
70% Med-Hi	7	400°F
80% Reheat	8	450°F
90–100% Hi	9–10	500°F

12

Why is there a temperature setting on a microwave oven?

A temperature setting is often used in conjunction with a Temperature Probe, which is a kind of thermometer. A Temperature Probe records the internal temperature of a food while it is cooking and automatically shuts off the oven when the temperature at which it is set is reached. A Probe records the food temperature and not the oven temperature. When cooking to the desired temperature be sure to always follow the recipe's covering and power level instructions. That will assure your food is fully cooked without being dried out.

13

What is a multi-stage program?

Microwave ovens can be programmed to do a multitude of cooking procedures automatically. Each oven has its own features which you can discover in your manual, but many can be set to move through the following steps:

- **Frozen casserole—**
  1st Stage—Defrost
  2nd Stage—Cook
  3rd Stage—Hold until ready to serve

- **Baking—**
  1st Stage—Begin baking process slowly
  2nd Stage—Quicken process by increasing the power level
  3rd Stage—Pause and test for doneness

- **White Sauce—**
  1st Stage—Melt butter
  2nd Stage—Cook added ingredients
  3rd Stage—Stir to prevent lumping

Multi-stage programming is a convenience so you can do all your programming in one step. Many models have memories in which you can store your most frequently used programs.

14

Will food brown in the microwave?

Yes! Meats cooked for more than 10 minutes will brown naturally. During cooking, the fat on the outside caramelizes and turns brown. The higher the fat content, the faster the meat will brown. For instance, bacon browns in one minute.

There are commercial products on the market to aid in browning those foods which need a little help! There are also many items in your kitchen which will aid in browning. Depending upon the food, many spices can be used to attain a browned color—soy sauce, worcestershire sauce, cinnamon, nutmeg, paprika, steak sauce, barbecue sauce, onion soup mixes, brown sugar, and corn syrup. But more about that in the recipe section.

A Browning Dish is required for foods with very short cooking times that need to be crisp or brown.

15

What should I know about reheating food?

• Always cover main dishes tightly. Reheat on High, if they have been refrigerated, until steaming hot.

• Stir a main dish, if possible, during reheating. If that cannot be done, rotate the dish while it is reheating.

• Reheat meats and layered main dishes at 50%. Meats should never be cooked beyond their original doneness. Layered casseroles need to be heated through, yet they can't be stirred, so lower power and longer reheating time works best.

• Begin heating frozen casseroles on High for 5 minutes. Stir, if possible, then reduce power to 50% and continue heating until food is steaming hot.

• To reheat a plate of food, place the denser foods (or the denser parts) to the outside and the more delicate or porous foods to the center. Cover with waxed paper or plastic. Heat at 80% for 3 minutes.

16

Do I need to buy new cookware for use in my microwave oven?

No! Most households have an array of cookware that can be used in the microwave oven. Glass, paper, and plastics are safe. If you are uncertain about a particular utensil, place a styrofoam cup full of water and the piece of cookware in question in the microwave oven. Microwave on High for one minute. If the water gets hot and the cookware remains at room temperature, it is suitable for microwave cooking.

Avoid metal cookware because it will reflect the microwaves rather than letting them penetrate. Avoid metallic trimmed cookware because energy can become trapped in the metal trim and cause arcing which appears as sparks and can cause a fire.

Aluminum trays can be used if they are less than ¾ inch deep and the foil cover is removed from the top. (If a metal tray is too deep, the energy can become trapped inside and cause a fire.) But insert the tray back into its cardboard package before placing it in the microwave to avoid metal touching metal. Never place a metal tray directly onto a metal rack.

17

Why do some microwave ovens have a metal rack?

A rack is to be used only when there is not enough space on the bottom of the oven to accommodate all the food to be cooked, or when foods need to be arranged for a varied cooking pattern. These racks are specifically designed with proper spacing for use in particular ovens so the microwave energy can pass through to each level.

18

How do I adapt my recipes for use in the microwave?

There are three basic ways to work at this:

1. Find a microwave recipe that is similar to your conventional recipe and use that instead.

2. Experiment! Because each kind of food requires particular handling in the microwave, it is best to consult the chapter in this book containing recipes and ingredients most like the one you want to convert. (For example, the introduction to Cakes on page 140 explains that less water and fewer eggs are needed in a microwave than in a conventional oven.)
Be sure to also check a parallel recipe's covering and power level instructions to be sure the food will not dry out or be over- or undercooked. Use a temperature probe to be sure the food reaches an internal temperature of 150°, thereby assuring that the food is fully cooked.

3. If all else fails, divide your conventional recipe's cooking time by 4, and experiment from there.
You should understand that converting recipes or multiplying or reducing a recipe's stated yield is always a bit of a gamble. Remember that because the number of microwaves in an oven is constant, larger amounts take longer than smaller portions. Experiment carefully, then record your successful results in the white space on the appropriate page.

A Quick Guide to Microwave Equipment

Glass Measure

This term refers to glass measuring cups with handles, that have graduations indicating measurements. The graduations are handy since you can measure and cook in the same container. The handle is helpful for removing extremely hot ingredients from the oven. The bowl will become very hot, but usually the handle remains cool enough to handle. This is especially useful when making candy. A deep measure is desirable for cooking foods that have a tendency to boil over. When purchasing look for 2-, 4-, and 8-cup sizes.

Glass Pie Pan

These usually come in 9- and 10-inch sizes. Both have their advantages. Omelets and pies work well in a 9-inch pan. Casseroles and meat need the larger space offered in the 10-inch size. This is a very versatile piece of equipment that is inexpensive and found on most cooks' shelves. It can double as a shallow casserole which can be covered with either waxed paper or plastic wrap.

Glass Baking Dish

Rectangular baking dishes are used to prepare a variety of foods. Be sure to check the size of your oven before purchasing any. If your oven has a carousel be sure the dish can turn. Choose a variety of sizes so you can cook the appropriate amounts for your household, as well as for larger groups when you have guests.

Covered Casseroles

Many kitchens are well equipped with a variety of usable casserole dishes. (If you need to stock up, a complete set can be purchased for about $20.) Many have interchangeable lids and stack for easy storage. Round casseroles give more even cooking results. Shallow casseroles allow for better cooking patterns, since the microwaves do not need to penetrate through as much food.

Baking Ring

This is a relatively inexpensive piece that you will quickly find indispensible. It produces even cooking patterns since it is round, and with the tube in the center it cooks from the inside out as well. Use it for just about anything that you want to cook quickly and efficiently. To substitute for it you can invert a glass tumbler in the middle of a round 3-quart casserole.

Meat Rack

Meat racks are available in a number of styles, shapes, and materials. Their purpose is to elevate the meat from its cooking juices. This can also be accomplished by inverting a saucer in a dish and laying the meat on the saucer. Meat racks are usually very inexpensive and a worthwhile purchase if you plan to cook a lot of meat. They work especially well for bacon.

Browning Dish

If you choose to purchase only one piece of equipment, it should probably be a browning dish. They come in a variety of shapes, sizes, and materials. Be sure you know your oven size and how you plan to use the dish before buying one. Having two different sizes is handy—a small one for quick breakfasts and lunches and a large one that covers the entire floor of the oven for doing larger quantities of food.

Plastic versus Glass

Both have their advantages and disadvantages. Glass breaks easily but cooks and cleans up well. Plastics are sometimes sensitive to extreme temperatures and will blister or melt. Plastic stains more easily than glass.

The Recipes

SAUCES

Sauces Are Simple in a Microwave

Sauces, and your favorite soups, casseroles, puddings, and pies that have sauces in them, are easily made in the microwave. No more endless stirring over a hot stove!

• Measure, cook, and serve all in the same cup.

• Only a minimal amount of stirring is necessary to distribute the heat and keep the starch in suspension.

• REMEMBER! Always prepare the sauce in a container twice the height of the sauce. That will prevent the sauce from boiling over as it cooks.

• Clean-up is easy because there are no scorched spots to scrub.

• The finished sauce is lump-free.

• Sauces that separate can be reblended in a mixer or blender.

• Sauces continue to thicken as they cool.

Basic White Sauce

Preparation Time: 5 minutes	Yields 1 cup

Microwave on High for 30 seconds in a 4-cup glass measuring cup:
> **2 tablespoons margarine**

Gradually stir in:
> **2 tablespoons flour**
> **1 cup warm milk**

Microwave on High for 2 minutes. Stir. Microwave on High another 2 minutes. Stir.

Note: Constant stirring is not necessary because the microwaves agitate the liquid, but it is important to stir occasionally to avoid lumps.

Basic Cheese Sauce

Preparation Time: 5 minutes	Yields 2 cups

Prepare Basic White Sauce. During final stirring blend in:
> **1 cup cheese, shredded**

Note: American cheese will give a creamy texture.
Cheddar cheese will produce a rich color and flavor.
A combination of cheeses works best and is a convenient way to use leftovers and ends that begin to dry out.

Note: This sauce works well poured over fresh broccoli and cauliflower or other vegetables.

Brown Almond Sauce

Preparation Time: 10 minutes   *Yields 1 cup*

Place in 4-cup glass measure:
3 tablespoons almonds, blanched
2 tablespoons butter
Microwave on High for 2 minutes, stirring twice during that time. Then stir in:
2 tablespoons flour
Microwave on High for 1 minute. Gradually stir in:
1 cup light cream or half and half
Microwave on High for 2 minutes. Stir. Microwave on High another 2 minutes. Stir.

Brown Mushroom Sauce

Preparation Time: 10 minutes   *Yields 1 cup*

Place in 4-cup glass measuring cup:
3 tablespoons fresh mushrooms, sliced
2 tablespoons butter
Microwave on High for 1 minute. Stir. Microwave on High for 1 minute more. Gently stir in:
2 tablespoons flour
Microwave on High for 1 minute. Gradually stir in:
1 cup light cream or half and half
Microwave on High for 2 minutes. Stir. Microwave on High for 2 more minutes. Stir.

Roux

Preparation Time: 2 minutes   *Yields 4 tablespoons*

Place in 2-cup glass measuring cup:
2 tablespoons butter
Microwave on High for 30 seconds. Stir in:
2 tablespoons flour
Microwave on High for 30 seconds to take away the raw flour taste.

Note: This can be whisked into any hot liquid to thicken it. Chicken, fish, beef or veal stock make tasty gravies.

White Sauce from Roux

Preparation Time: 5 minutes   Yields 1 cup

Heat in 4-cup glass measure:
>**1 cup milk**

Whisk in:
>**4 tablespoons Roux**

Microwave on High for 2 minutes. Stir. Microwave on High another 2 minutes.

Note: White sauce may also be referred to as Bechamel.

Note: For a richer sauce use cream instead of milk.

Cheese Sauce from Roux

Preparation Time: 5 minutes   Yields 2 cups

Prepare Bechamel or White Sauce as directed above.
Whisk in:
>**1 cup cheese, shredded**

Season with salt, pepper, and dry mustard to taste.

Quick Sauces

Canned soups make very quick sauces. They can be served undiluted, or for a richer sauce they can be diluted with cream or stock. Pour into glass measuring cup and microwave on High for 3-6 minutes
Processed cheese spreads melt very quickly. They can be melted in their jars on High in about 1 minute.

Mornay Sauce

Preparation Time: 10 minutes   *Yields 1½ cups*

Place in 4-cup glass measure:
> **2 tablespoons butter**
> **½ teaspoon onion, minced**

Microwave on High for 2 minutes. Stir in:
> **2 tablespoons flour**
> **1 cup milk**

Microwave on High for 2 minutes. Stir. Microwave on High another 2 minutes. Gradually whisk in:
> **1 egg yolk**
> **2 tablespoons heavy cream**

Microwave on High for 45 seconds, stirring twice during that time. Stir in:
> **2 tablespoons parmesan cheese**
> **¼ cup gruyere or swiss cheese, grated**

Stir to melt cheese, then serve over eggs, chicken, fish, or vegetables.

Hollandaise Sauce

Preparation Time: 4–5 minutes   *Yields 1 cup*

Note: This Sauce has a tendency to curdle so be sure to microwave for only 15 seconds at a time, then stir, alternating those steps until the Sauce is finished.

In a small glass bowl combine:
> **3 eggs yolks**
> **4½ teaspoons lemon juice**
> **dash red pepper sauce**
> **dash white pepper**

In 2-cup microwave-safe measuring cup, microwave on High for 45 seconds:
> **½ cup butter**

Whisk into egg mixture and microwave on High for 15 seconds. Repeat the whisking and microwaving process 4 to 6 times or until the sauce resembles heavy cream. Season to taste with salt and serve immediately.

Note: For an interesting twist, substitute 3 tablespoons freshly squeezed orange juice and ½ teaspoon finely grated rind for the lemon.

• Additional recipes in this collection which use Sauces and the techniques described here are:

EGGS AND CHEESES

The Advantages of Cooking Eggs in a Microwave

- Prepare, cook, and serve all in the same container.
- One egg cooks in 45–60 seconds!
- Eggs, properly microwaved, are light, fluffy, and moist.
- ALWAYS pierce the yolk and remove the egg from its shell before micro-waving to prevent its exploding from internal pressure.
- ALWAYS cover an egg to trap the steam for even cooking and to protect your oven from splashes. A tight-fitting lid or plastic wrap produces the best results.
- It is best to microwave an egg at 70% power (rather than on High) since eggs are high in protein and so have a tendency to toughen at high temperatures.
- Don't overcook an egg. It should still look wet at the end of the sug-gested cooking time. Allow it to stand before cooking it longer. Because the cooking time is so short, you may need to experiment before finding the ideal cooking time for you. Make a note of what you discover works best.

Scrambled in a Cup

Scramble in a microwave-safe cup:
> **1 egg, yolk pierced**
> **dash red pepper sauce**

Cover with lid or plastic wrap.
Microwave at 70% for 1 minute. If the egg is not done to your liking, microwave in 10-second intervals until it is.
Note here how long it takes.
Season and serve.

Poached Eggs

Place in 6-ounce custard cup:
> **¼ cup water**
> **⅛ teaspoon vinegar**

Slip in:
> **1 egg, yolk pierced**

Cover with lid or plastic wrap. Microwave on High (water absorbs extra power) for 1 minute. Season and serve.

Hard-Cooked Eggs for Slicing

Create your own round containers by cutting the cardboard cylinder from a paper towel roll into quarters, thus making four short cylinders. Line each with plastic wrap. Then stand each on end and break an egg into each container. Pierce the yolks with a wooden toothpick. Cover the top of each cylinder with plastic wrap. Microwave at 50% for 2 minutes. Check for doneness.
If it is not necessary that the finished egg be round for slicing, crack the egg into a lightly greased custard cup. Cover with plastic wrap and microwave at 50% for 2 minutes. Check for doneness.

Baked Egg

Place in 10-ounce custard cup:

> **½ teaspoon butter, melted**
> **1 egg, yolk pierced**

Cover with plastic wrap. Microwave at 70% for 45 seconds. Allow to stand for 1 minute.

Fried Egg

Preheat browning dish according to manufacturer's directions. Add:

> **½ teaspoon butter**
> **1 egg, yolk pierced**

Cover with dish lid. Microwave at 70% for 45 seconds. Season and serve.

Easy Omelet

Preparation Time: 7 minutes   *2 servings*

Combine in 9-inch microwave-safe pie plate:

> **4 eggs**
> **⅛ teaspoon salt**
> **dash red pepper sauce**

Cover with plastic wrap. Microwave at 70% for 4 minutes.
Fill with favorite filling (see suggestions below).
Microwave on High for 30 seconds to 1 minute to warm filling.
Filling suggestions:

> **bacon, crumbled**
> **broccoli and cauliflower, lightly cooked**
> **cheese, grated**
> **ham, cooked and cubed**
> **mushrooms**
> **onions and peppers, chopped**
> **sausage, browned and crumbled**
> **tomatoes, onions, and peppers, chopped**
> **any leftovers**

Puffy Omelet

Preparation Time: 25 minutes	4 servings

Microwave on High for 1–2 minutes in 2-quart microwave-safe casserole:

¼ cup butter

Stir in:

¼ cup all-purpose flour
½ teaspoon salt
dash red pepper sauce
1 cup milk, adding it gradually after other ingredients are mixed in

Microwave on High for 3–5 minutes or until bubbly. Stir every minute during cooking time.

Stir in until melted:

1 cup cheese, shredded

Stir in:

1 cup chopped broccoli, cooked

Beat slightly and add slowly to vegetable mixture:

4 egg yolks

Using clean beaters, beat until stiff peaks form and then gently fold in:

4 egg whites

Microwave covered at 50% for 14–18 minutes or until set in the center. Serve warm.

Note: Substitute your favorite fillings. This is a convenient way to use leftovers.

Croissant Breakfast Sandwich

Preparation Time: 10 minutes   *4 servings*

Beat together in 1-quart glass measuring bowl:
3 eggs
3 tablespoons milk or water
Microwave on High for 3–3½ minutes or until nearly set. Cut in half horizontally:
4 baked croissants
Combine and then spread on each croissant:
2 tablespoons mayonnaise
1 teaspoon prepared mustard
Top with a slice of:
ham or canadian bacon
Spoon on egg mixture and top with other half of croissant.
Place on a microwave-safe plate and cover with paper towel or napkin.
Microwave on High for 30–60 seconds or until heated through.

Denver Pockets

Preparation Time: 11 minutes   *4 servings*

Combine in 1-quart microwave-safe casserole:
1 small onion, chopped
¼ cup green pepper, chopped
1 tablespoon butter
Microwave on High for 2–3 minutes or until tender.
Stir in:
½ cup ham, cubed and cooked
3 eggs, beaten
⅛ teaspoon salt
dash pepper
Microwave on High for 2–2½ minutes or until eggs are set.
Cut in half to form 4 pockets:
2 6-inch pita breads
Fill each pocket with ½ cup egg mixture and sprinkle with:
shredded cheese
Microwave on High for 30–45 seconds to melt cheese.

Crab Quiche

Preparation Time: 30 minutes   *6 servings*

Combine:
> **1 cup unsifted all-purpose flour**
> **½ teaspoon salt**

Cut in, until mixture resembles coarse crumbs:
> **⅓ cup shortening**

In separate container combine:
> **2–3 tablespoons cold water**
> **2 drops yellow food coloring**

Gradually stir into flour mixture until dough clings together. Form into a smooth ball.

Roll out onto floured, cloth-covered surface to circle one inch larger than 9-inch glass pie plate. Fit into pie plate. Fold under edge, forming standing rim. Flute. Prick bottom and sides with fork. Weight with dried rice, beans, or a casserole dish. Microwave uncovered on High for 4–5 minutes or until crust is no longer doughy, rotating plate twice. Set crust aside.

Place in 1-cup glass measure:
> **1 cup half and half cream**

Microwave on High 2–2½ minutes or until steaming hot.

In separate container beat together:
> **4 eggs**
> **1 teaspoon chopped chives**
> **1 teaspoon dijon-style mustard**
> **½ teaspoon salt**
> **dash of pepper**
> **dash of nutmeg**

Slowly beat in hot cream.

Layer in crust:
> **6 ounces crabmeat**
> **¾ cup (3 ounces) shredded swiss cheese**

Pour egg mixture into crust. Cover with waxed paper.

Microwave on High for 7–9 minutes or until center is almost set, rotating dish two or three times.

Note: Other unbaked 9-inch pastry shells can be used. Prick with fork and microwave as directed. Frozen or canned shrimp can be substituted for crab.

Quiche

Preparation Time: 20 minutes   *6–8 servings*

Microwave in glass pie plate on High for 4–5 minutes or until no longer doughy:

9-inch pastry shell, pricked and weighted with smaller dish

Microwave on High for 4–5 minutes in glass bowl:

1 small onion, chopped
4 slices bacon, chopped

Stir in:

2 tablespoons flour
½ teaspoon salt
dash red pepper sauce

Beat in:

2 eggs
1¼ cup half and half or light cream
¼ cup cheese, shredded

Pour into prepared pastry shell. Cover loosely with plastic wrap. Microwave on High for 6–8 minutes or until center is set. Let stand 10 minutes. Garnish with chopped chives or parsley.

Pizza Quiche

Preparation time: 25 minutes   *6–8 servings*

Crumble into 9-inch glass pie plate, then microwave on High for 5–6 minutes:

1 pound ground beef
1 medium onion, chopped

Drain fat and stir in:

½ teaspoon salt
¼ teaspoon pepper
1 teaspoon mustard

Combine in blender and pour over cooked meat:

1¼ cups milk
¾ cup buttermilk baking mix
3 eggs

Microwave on High for 6 minutes or until edges are set; then microwave at 50% for 4–6 minutes or until center is set.

Top with:

      2 tomatoes, sliced
      1 cup cheese, shredded
      paprika

Microwave on High for 1–3 minutes or until cheese is melted. Cut into wedges.
Serve warm.

Note: For more pizza flavor substitute 1 cup pizza sauce for tomatoes and microwave on High for 5–6 minutes.

Sausage Quiche

Preparation Time: 25 minutes   *6 servings*

Microwave on High for 4–5 minutes or until no longer doughy:
      9-inch pastry shell, pricked and weighted
Microwave on High for 2–3 minutes in microwaveable colander combination:
      ½ pound pork sausage, removed from casing
      ¾ cup fresh mushrooms, sliced
      ¼ cup onion, chopped
      ¼ cup green pepper, chopped
      1 clove garlic, minced
Drain and sprinkle over bottom of partially cooked pie shell.
Combine and pour over sausage mixture:
      2 tablespoons flour
      ½ teaspoon salt
      ¼ teaspoon pepper
      2 eggs
      1¼ cups light cream
Top with:
      ¾ cup mozzarella cheese
      ¼ cup parmesan cheese
      2 tablespoons parsley, snipped
Cover with plastic wrap. Microwave on High for 6–8 minutes or until center is almost set.

Swiss Cheese Fondue

Preparation Time: 15 minutes   *Yields*   *3 cups*

Combine in 1½-quart glass casserole:

        3 tablespoons all-purpose flour
        ¼ teaspoon salt
        ⅛ teaspoon white pepper
        1 cup milk

Beat with rotary beater or wire whisk until smooth. Stir in:

        1 pound swiss cheese, shredded

Add:

        1 tablespoon butter or margarine

Cover with glass lid. Microwave at 70% for 5 minutes. Stir well. Microwave at 70% for 5–6 minutes or until thickened and smooth (about 180°F). Stir in:

        ½ cup white cooking wine
        dash of nutmeg

Serve warm from fondue pot or chafing dish with French bread cubes or bread sticks. May be made ahead, refrigerated and reheated. To reheat, microwave at 70% for about 8 minutes, or until warm (about 120°F). Stir well before serving.

• Additional recipes in this collection which use Eggs and Cheese and the techniques described here are:

        Night-Before Sausage Brunch, page 97
        Potato Brunch, page 56
        Vanilla Custard, page 174
        Chocolate Custard, page 174
        Floating Island, page 173
        Pumpkin Custard, page 175
        Vanilla Custard Ice Cream, page 176
        Chocolate Custard Ice Cream, page 176
        Lemon Meringue Pie, page 164
        Lemon Chiffon Pie, page 164
        Coconut Cream Pie, page 165
        Coconut Custard Pie, page 166
        Pumpkin Pie Bake, page 166

VEGETABLES AND SALADS

Microwaved Vegetables Are Beautifully Healthful

• Vegetables cooked in a microwave retain their color, shape, and nutrients due to their shortened cooking time and waterless cooking.

• Most vegetables can be cooked in their natural form. Rinse off their surface dirt to clean them, but also to supply additional moisture for cooking.

• Whenever possible, prepare vegetables so the pieces are uniform in size. That will assure more even cooking.

• If you choose to cook vegetables whole, that also works well. Simply extend the cooking time because of the greater density.

• If certain parts of a vegetable are more dense than others (the stem ends of asparagus or broccoli, for example), lay the denser ends toward the outside edge of the dish so they are hit first by the microwaves.

• Whenever possible, cook vegetables in their serving dish, covering them with plastic wrap or a tight-fitting lid.

• Cook on High unless indicated otherwise. Because most vegetables have a high water content, they turn out well when done at that power level.

Artichokes

Trim off stem and 1 inch off top. Brush with lemon juice. Wrap in waxed paper. Microwave on High for 4–6 minutes apiece.

Asparagus

Due to the fibrous stems, asparagus needs water to cook. When preparing spears, stand them in a small amount of water and cover with plastic wrap, or arrange them in a circle lying flat, so the tips are to the center and the stems to the outside. Microwave on High for 6–8 minutes per pound.

Broccoli

Fresh broccoli should be rinsed and cut into uniform pieces. Place in covered casserole and microwave on High for 5 minutes per pound. Trim away any portions that have become dehydrated.

Beans (Green and Lima)

Beans require extra moisture for even cooking. They work very nicely in casseroles. To prepare alone, cover bottom of casserole with water and shield top with foil. This will cause the water on the bottom to steam the beans before the microwaves cook them on top. Microwave on High for 5–10 minutes per pound.

Beets

Dice or slice into uniform pieces. Because beets are fibrous they require cooking in water or flavored juice. Place in covered casserole with desired liquid and microwave on High for 5–7 minutes per pound.

Brussels Sprouts

Rinse sprouts and remove excess leaves. Combine 1 pound fresh sprouts in covered casserole with ¼ cup water. Microwave on High for 10–12 minutes or until tender.

Cabbage

Shredded cabbage cooks faster than a whole head. Save the outer leaves for stuffing with a meat or vegetable mixture. Cut remainder of 1-pound head into wedges. Place in baking dish with ¼ cup water and microwave on High for 12–15 minutes. Or shred cabbage, place in baking dish with ¼ cup water and microwave on High for 7–12 minutes. To retain color, add a splash of lemon juice or vinegar to the cabbage before microwaving.

Carrots

Dice or slice into uniform pieces. Because carrots are fibrous they require cooking in ¼ cup water or other liquid. Place in covered casserole with desired liquid and microwave on High for 5–7 minutes per pound.

Cauliflower

Cauliflower can be cooked whole or broken into flowerettes. Rinse off surface dirt. Wrap in plastic wrap or place in covered casserole. Cook flowerettes on High for about 5 minutes per pound. Cooking a whole 1-pound head on High will take 6–9 minutes.

Corn on the Cob

This is the easiest vegetable of all to prepare because it is in its natural wrapper. Just microwave in the husk on High for 3 minutes per ear. Don't do more than six at a time. They will stay warm in the husk for 30 minutes while you attend to other matters. Be careful not to steam yourself when you husk them because they stay hot.

Corn Kernels

Place 2 cups kerneled corn in baking dish with 2 tablespoons water. Cover tightly. Microwave on High for 4–7 minutes.

Eggplant

For crisp eggplant, peel, then thinly slice it, dip each slice in egg wash and then into fresh bread crumbs. Preheat browning dish, add a small amount of oil, and brown to desired crispness.

Mushrooms

Wash and slice, chop or stuff. Saute with a small amount of butter by microwaving on High for 3–6 minutes, stirring after 2 minutes. Or stuff with anything you like and arrange in a circle on a paper plate. Microwave on High for about 1 minute per plate.

Onions

Cook whole, sliced, or chopped. Onions are very flavorful when cooked mainly in their natural juices. Place whole, along with 2 tablespoons water, in 1½-quart casserole. Cover tightly. Microwave on High for 7–8 minutes. Or place 1 pound sliced onions, along with 2 tablespoons water, in 1½-quart casserole. Cover tightly. Microwave on High for 6–7 minutes.

Peas

Combine 2 cups fresh peas with ¼ cup water in covered casserole. Microwave on High for 7–8 minutes.
Frozen peas cook very nicely in the box or pouch. Pierce and microwave on High for 4–6 minutes for 10-ounce package.

Peppers

Peppers can be sauteed in their own juices. Rinse with water, remove stem, seeds, and membrane. Slice or chop to desired size. Place in microwave-safe dish and microwave to desired doneness. Start on High, checking every 30 seconds for doneness.

Potatoes

A potato's size, type, and moisture all affect its cooking time. For example, a round potato takes longer to cook than an oval one.

Scrub potatoes to remove surface dirt. Pierce in several places to allow steam to escape. Arrange in a circle, spoke fashion. For a crisper shell grease the potatoes. Turn over halfway through cooking time for more even cooking. Microwave on High for 3–5 minutes for each potato being cooked. Allow 5 minutes standing time. Potatoes will stay warm for 45 minutes if they are wrapped in foil or placed in a basket and covered. There are many uses for leftover potatoes:

• Slice or cube and brown in butter on browning dish.
• Cut in half and scoop out centers. Use for mashed potatoes or mix with cheese and bacon and restuff.
• Fill shells with creamed vegetables, chili, cheese, or other fillings.
• Cooked potatoes peel easily and are a good source of vitamins and minerals. They are extremely tasty when used for soups or salads.

Spinach

Wash thoroughly, then cover, and microwave on High for 4–6 minutes per pound.

Squash

Squash can be cooked whole, sliced, or diced. To cook whole, pierce skin in several places and place on paper plate, Microwave on High to desired doneness. You may want to partially cook it, then scoop out the pulp and finish cooking it at mealtime. When preparing squash for freezing, cook until the pulp is tender, then puree it and freeze for later use.

Sweet Potatoes and Yams

Scrub and pierce skins of:
> **5 sweet potatoes, 5–6 ounces each**

Arrange in spoke fashion on round baking tray or plate. Microwave on High for 10 minutes. When cool enough to handle, peel and slice into 2-quart glass casserole.

Combine in 2-cup glass measuring cup:
> **1 cup brown sugar**
> **⅓ cup water**
> **2 tablespoons butter**
> **½ teaspoon salt**

Microwave on High for 2 minutes. Stir. Microwave on High another 2 minutes. Pour over potatoes in casserole. Microwave on High for 6–8 more minutes.

Note: Add your favorite ingredients to brighten the flavor: raisins, chopped apples, nuts, marshmallows, pineapples, or apricots.

When Blanching Vegetables:

- Use top quality vegetables.
- Clean and prepare as for cooking.
- Cut into uniform pieces.
- Blanch in container without water (and thus avoid the mess of draining).
- Chill in same container.
- Seal, label, date, and freeze.
- Reheat in same container.

Blanching Chart

Vegetable	Amount	Time
Asparagus (cut in 1-inch pieces)	4 cups	4½ minutes in ¼ cup water
Beans	1 pound	5 minutes
Broccoli (cut in 2-inch pieces)	1 pound	5½ minutes
Carrots (sliced)	1 pound	5 minutes
Cauliflower (flowerettes)	1 head	6 minutes
Corn (cut from cob)	4 cups	4 minutes
Peas	4 cups	4½ minutes
Spinach (washed)	1 pound	4½ minutes
Zucchini (sliced or cubed)	1 pound	4 minutes

Green Bean Bake

Preparation Time: 15 minutes   *4 servings*

Combine in 2-quart casserole:
> **20 ounces green beans, frenched and frozen**
> **1 can cream of mushroom soup, condensed**

Cover and microwave on High for 9 minutes.
Stir in:
> **1 can french fried onion rings (reserve a few for garnish)**

Microwave on High for 3 minutes.

Baked Beans a la Microwave

Preparation Time: 15 minutes   *6–8 servings*

Place in 1½-quart glass casserole, cover with paper towel, and microwave on High for 4 minutes or until crisp:
> **4 slices bacon**

Remove bacon and crumble.
Stir into drippings, along with crumbled bacon:
> **1 cup catsup**
> **2 cans beans (mix any you like)**
> **½ cup brown sugar**
> **1 tablespoon mustard**
> **1 tablespoon worcestershire sauce**

Cover. Microwave on High for 7–8 minutes or until heated through.

Canned Beans with Pork

Preparation Time: 6 minutes   *2–3 servings*

Place contents of 16-ounce can in covered casserole and microwave on High for 4–6 minutes.

Broccoli and Cauliflower with Cheese Sauce

Preparation Time: 20 minutes   *6–8 servings*

Arrange on 10-inch glass baking platter:

1 pound cauliflower flowerettes
1 pound broccoli flowerettes

Decorate with:

red pepper rings or
pimento or
cherry tomatoes

Cover with plastic wrap. Microwave on High for 10–12 minutes. Immediately uncover, being careful of steam.

Prepare Cheese Sauce by microwaving in 4-cup glass measure for 30 seconds:

2 tablespoons margarine

Stir in:

2 tablespoons flour
1 cup warm milk

Microwave on High for 2 minutes. Stir. Microwave on High for 2 more minutes. Stir in:

1 cup cheddar cheese, shredded

Pour over broccoli and cauliflower.

Note: Add white sauce to leftovers to create a cream soup, or add a package of stuffing mix and white sauce to leftovers to make a casserole.

Broccoli and Cauliflower Italiano

Preparation Time: 15 minutes   *6–8 servings*

Arrange on 10-inch glass baking platter:

1 pound cauliflower flowerettes
1 pound broccoli flowerettes

Decorate with:

red pepper rings or
pimento or
cherry tomatoes

Top with:

italian dressing

Cover with plastic wrap and microwave on High for 10–12 minutes.

Eggplant Parmesan

Preparation Time: 20 minutes	6 servings

Combine in small bowl:
> **¼ cup bread crumbs**
> **¼ cup parmesan cheese**
> **2 tablespoon butter, melted**

Layer in 1½-quart casserole:
> **1 medium eggplant, sliced and peeled**
> **bread crumb mixture**
> **2 cups spaghetti sauce** (see page 88)
> **2 cups mozzarella cheese, grated**

Cover with casserole lid and microwave on High and to internal temperature of 150°F, about 15 minutes.

Sausage-Stuffed Mushrooms

Preparation Time: 20 minutes	Yields 25–30 mushrooms

Wash:
> **1 pound large fresh mushrooms**

Twist stems from each cap.
Crumble into glass casserole:
> **1 pound italian sausage**

Microwave on High for 4 minutes. Drain excess fat. Combine sausage with:
> **8 ounces cream cheese, softened**

Fill each mushroom with sausage mixture. Arrange stuffed mushroom caps on heat resistant platter or paper plate. Microwave at 70% for 5–6 minutes or until hot. Serve hot.

Stuffed Peppers

Preparation Time: 30 minutes   6 servings

Cut off tops and remove centers from:
> **6 medium-sized peppers**

In mixing bowl combine:
> **1 pound ground beef**
> **1 small onion, chopped**
> **1 cup rice, uncooked**
> **2 cups tomato sauce**
> **2 cups water**

Stuff peppers and mound with filling.
Place in deep 3-quart casserole with lid.
Microwave at 80% about 25 minutes or until peppers are tender and filling is set.

Mashed Potatoes

Pare and cube potatoes, add a small amount of water, cover tightly, and microwave on High for 3 minutes for each medium-sized potato. Season with salt, pepper and butter. Mash to desired consistency, adding warmed milk.

Scalloped Potatoes

Butter casserole, layer sliced potatoes with butter, salt, and pepper, then cover and microwave on High for 3 minutes for each medium potato used, or until potatoes are tender.

Scalloped Potatoes with White Sauce

Precook potatoes. Slice and layer in buttered casserole. Pour Basic White Sauce (see page 27) or Cheese Sauce (see page 27) over potatoes and microwave at 70% for 4–6 minutes, or until potatoes are heated through. For a crisp crust, top with buttered bread crumbs or crushed cereal crumbs. Be sure to use an extra large casserole to prevent cooking over.

Scalloped Potatoes and Ham

Combine in covered 1½ quart-casserole, then microwave on High for 8–9 minutes:

4 cups potatoes, sliced
1 small onion, sliced
½ cup water

Melt in 4-cup glass measure on High for 30 seconds:

2 tablespoons butter

Stir in:

2 tablespoons flour
1 cup milk, added gradually
1 teaspoon parsley
½ teaspoon salt
¼ teaspoon dry mustard
⅛ teaspoon pepper

Microwave on High for 2 minutes. Stir. Microwave on High another 2 minutes. Stir in:

1 cup cubed ham

Pour over potatoes. Sprinkle with paprika. Microwave on High for 5–6 minutes.

Potato Stuffing

Preparation Time: 15 minutes   *4 servings*

Combine in 9 × 13 baking dish:

½ cup butter
1 small onion, chopped

Microwave on High for 2 minutes. Add:

4 potatoes, peeled and cubed

Cover with plastic wrap and microwave on High for 10 minutes. Stir in:

2 cups croutons or stuffing mix

Potato Brunch

Preparation Time: 15 minutes   6 servings

Place in shallow 2-quart covered casserole dish:
Microwave on High for 6–7 minutes:
12-ounce package hash browns
Combine in 1-quart glass measure and pour over potatoes:
6 eggs
⅓ cup whipping cream
1 cup cheddar cheese, grated
2 tablespoons chives, chopped
¼ teaspoon salt
dash pepper
1 cup ham, cubed
Microwave on High for 3–4 minutes. Stir. Microwave 2 more minutes. Stir.
Microwave again until eggs are set, being careful not to overcook them.

Note: Other fully-cooked meats can be substituted for ham, like: canadian bacon, cooked pork roll, or cooked sausage.

Stuffed Tomatoes

Cut tops off and scoop out:
6 medium tomatoes
Chop the centers and combine with:
1 cup bread crumbs
2 eggs
½ cup butter, melted
1 tablespoon parsley, minced
1 tablespoon onion, minced
1 teaspoon paprika
salt and pepper to taste
Stuff and mound filling in tomatoes. Arrange in circle on microwave-safe platter. Microwave at 70% for about 10 minutes, or until stuffing is puffy. Do not overcook.

Antipasto Jar

Preparation Time: 30 minutes   Yields   10–12 cups

Microwave on High for 4 minutes. Stir, then microwave on High another

4–6 minutes or until pickling liquid boils:

> **2 cups water**
> **1 cup cider vinegar**
> **2 tablespoons salt**
> **2 tablespoons vegetable oil**

Set pickling liquid aside.
Select 6 cups fresh vegetables:

> **broccoli, sliced**
> **brussels sprouts, halved**
> **carrots, sliced**
> **cauliflower, sliced**
> **squash, sliced**

Cover and cook on High for 4–8 minutes. Chill. Then select 2 cups of fresh vegetables:

> **green peppers, sliced**
> **olives**
> **cucumbers, sliced**
> **small mushrooms**
> **cherry tomatoes**

Mix with cooled, cooked vegetables and pack in canning jars. Pour pickling liquid over vegetables. Cover and refrigerate 2 to 3 days before serving. Store in the refrigerator no longer than 1 month. Take advantage of fresh vegetables and use as hostess gifts!

Greek Salad

Preparation Time: 20 minutes   *8 servings*

Microwave **1 lemon** on High for 20 seconds before squeezing to release more juice.
Combine:

> **½ cup plain yogurt**
> **½ cup mayonnaise**
> **1 tablespoon lemon juice**
> **1 teaspoon dill**

Pour over:

> **6 cups mixed greens**
> **1 red onion, sliced**
> **½ cucumber, sliced**
> **1 tomato, chopped**
> **½ cup feta cheese**
> **¼ cup olives, sliced**

Potato Salad

Preparation Time: 40 minutes   *10 servings*

Scrub 6 medium-sized potatoes, then pierce each in several places to allow steam to escape. Arrange them in a circle, spoke-fashion. Microwave on High for 20–25 minutes, turning each over halfway through cooking time. Let them stand for 5 minutes. Peel and cube. Mix gently with:

1 small onion, chopped fine
1 cup celery, chopped
1 teaspoon celery seed
1 teaspoon salt
4 hard-cooked eggs, diced (see page 35)

Fold in Potato Salad Dressing.

Potato Salad Dressing

Preparation Time: 10 minutes   *Yield 2½–3 cups*

Mix together:

2 eggs, well beaten
¾ cup sugar
1 teaspoon cornstarch
salt to taste
¼–½ cup apple cider vinegar
½ cup cream or evaporated milk
1 teaspoon mustard
3 tablespoons butter

Microwave on High for 2 minutes. Stir. Microwave on High another 2 minutes. Stir. Microwave on High 2 more minutes. Continue that process until mixture thickens. Then stir in until smooth:

1 cup mayonnaise

Spinach Salad

Preparation Time: 15 minutes	6–8 servings

Place in glass baking dish and cover with paper towel:
> **2 slices bacon**

Microwave on High for 3 minutes or until crisp. Remove bacon. Save drippings. Crumble bacon, then toss with:
> **12 ounces fresh spinach, cleaned and torn into small pieces**
> **2 cups lettuce, shredded**
> **6 green onions, sliced**
> **3 hard-cooked eggs, chopped**

Top with dressing made by combining in 1-cup glass measure and microwaving on High for 2 minutes:
> **¼ cup mayonnaise**
> **2 tablespoons sugar**
> **2 tablespoons vinegar**
> **bacon drippings**

Sweet and Sour Dressing

Preparation Time: 5 minutes	Yields 1 cup

In a two-cup glass measure, microwave on High for 15 seconds:
> **1 tablespoon butter**

Add:
> **1 tablespoon flour**
> **1 tablespoon prepared mustard**
> **¼ teaspoon salt**

Blend well. Stir in:
> **½ cup sugar**

Slowly blend in:
> **½ cup vinegar**
> **1 egg, beaten**

Microwave on High for 2–3 minutes, stirring after each minute, until mixture becomes very thick. Cool and chill before using. Dressing can be thinned with fruit juice to serve on fruit salad.

• Additional Recipes in this collection using **Vegetables** and the processes described here are:
> **Bean Soup**, page 65
> **French Onion Soup**, page 65
> **Potato Soup**, page 64

SOUPS

Hearty and Rich, Quick or Simmering

• A microwave oven can produce quick soups, especially if you work with canned bases and leftover vegetables or meats.

• A microwave oven can also simmer a several-hour soup if you like. For stock-based soups, especially beef or chicken, do not expect a speedy shortcut. Instead, because of the large volume of water needed, such a stew requires as much time as a conventional stove.

• The recipes presented in this section can be easily adapted to your favorite ingredients. Simply use the procedure that fits with the particular kinds of elements you've chosen.

Cream of Broccoli Soup

Preparation Time: 10 minutes   *4 servings*

Microwave on High for 30 seconds:

2 tablespoons margarine

Stir in:

2 tablespoons flour
1 cup warm milk

Microwave on High for 2 minutes. Stir. Microwave on High for 2 more minutes. Stir in:

10-ounce package of broccoli, defrosted

Microwave on High for 3 minutes. Stir. Microwave on High another 2–3 minutes until steaming.

Hominy Clam Chowder

Preparation Time: 20 minutes   *5–6 servings*

Place in single layer in 2-quart glass casserole:

2 slices bacon

Cover with paper towel.
Microwave on High for 2–3 minutes or until crisp. Remove bacon and set aside.
Add to drippings:

1 medium onion, chopped

Cover with casserole lid.
Microwave on High for 2–3 minutes or until tender.
Stir in:

¼ cup flour
3 cups half and half cream

Add:

1 can (20 ounces) white hominy, drained
2 cans (6½ ounces each) minced clams, undrained
½ teaspoon salt
⅛ teaspoon pepper
5 drops tabasco sauce

Microwave uncovered on High for 9–10 minutes or until mixture boils and thickens, stirring three or four times. Garnish with crumbled bacon.

Note: 2 tablespoons cooking oil or melted butter can be substituted for bacon drippings. A 16-ounce can of cut corn, drained, can be substituted for hominy. Chowder also can be made with half clams and half canned shrimp. Drain and rinse shrimp before adding to soup.

Potato Soup

Preparation Time: 35 minutes	4–6 servings

Place in single layer in 2-quart glass casserole:
> **3 slices bacon**

Cover with paper towel. Microwave on High for 3–4½ minutes or until bacon is crisp. Remove bacon and set aside.

Add to bacon drippings:
> **4 medium potatoes, cubed**
> **1 small onion, chopped**
> **1 cup celery, chopped**
> **2 cups water**
> **1½ teaspoons salt**
> **⅛ teaspoon pepper**

Cover with casserole lid. Microwave on High for 12–13 minutes or until vegetables are nearly tender.

In a separate container, combine until smooth:
> **5 tablespoons flour**
> **2 cups milk**

Stir into vegetable mixture. Microwave uncovered on High for 11–12 minutes or until mixture boils and thickens, stirring 2 or 3 times during last half of cooking time. Crumble bacon and use to garnish soup.

Home-Cooked Chicken and Broth

Preparation Time: 80 minutes	Yields 5 cups broth, 4 cups chicken

Combine in 3- or 4-quart glass casserole:
> **3–3½ pounds chicken pieces**
> **5 cups water**
> **1 large onion, chopped**
> **½ cup carrot, chopped**
> **½ cup celery, sliced**
> **1 bay leaf**
> **1 tablespoon salt**
> **⅛ teaspoon pepper**

Cover with casserole lid. Microwave on High for 18–20 minutes or until mixture begins to boil. Rearrange chicken pieces. Cover.

Microwave at 50% for 50–60 minutes or until chicken is tender. Remove chicken and use as desired. Use broth for soups. If desired, skim fat from broth and strain to remove vegetable pieces.

Bean Soup

Preparation Time: 3 hours	8 servings

Combine in 4–5-quart covered casserole:

1 pound dried beans, washed and sorted
8 cups water
2 teaspoons salt
2 teaspoons baking soda

Microwave on High for 18–20 minutes or until boiling. Let stand covered 1 hour.
Stir in:

1 ham shank
1 large onion, sliced
1 bay leaf
1–6 oz. can tomato paste
¼ teaspoon pepper

Microwave on High for 75–90 minutes. Serve hot.
Note: This recipe freezes well.

French Onion Soup

Preparation Time: 15 minutes	4–6 servings

Microwave in 3-quart casserole for 4 minutes:

¼ cup butter
1 large sweet onion, thinly sliced and separated

Stir in and microwave on High for 4–6 minutes:

1 20-ounce can beef broth
1 beef bouillon cube
1 teaspoon salt
⅓ cup dry red wine (optional)
salt and pepper

Divide into mugs or soup bowls and top with:

melba toast rounds
shredded gruyere cheese

Microwave on High for 1 minute to melt cheese.

Country Minestrone

Preparation Time: 35 minutes   6–8 servings

Combine in 3-quart glass casserole:
> **5 cups water**
> **1 can (10½ ounces) condensed beef bouillon**
> **5 teaspoons instant beef bouillon granules**
> **1 clove garlic, finely chopped**
> **1 small onion, chopped**
> **1 can (16 ounces) tomatoes, undrained**
> **1 cup broken, uncooked spaghetti pieces**
> **1 teaspoon salt**
> **⅛ teaspoon pepper**
> **¼ teaspoon leaf oregano**
> **¼ teaspoon leaf basil**

Cover with casserole lid. Microwave on High for 22–25 minutes or until spaghetti is tender.
Add:
> **1 cup frozen peas**
> **1 can (16 ounces) kidney beans**

Cover. Microwave on High for 5–6 minutes, or until heated through. If desired, sprinkle individual servings with shredded mozzarella cheese just before serving.

Sassy Tomato Soup for Two

Preparation Time: 6 minutes   2–3 servings

Combine in 4-cup glass measure:
> **1½ cups tomato juice**
> **1 can (10½ ounces) condensed beef consomme**
> **½ bay leaf**
> **dash of tabasco**
> **1 tablespoon sugar**
> **1 teaspoon parsley flakes**
> **dash pepper**
> **½ teaspoon worcestershire sauce, if desired**

Microwave uncovered on High for 5–6 minutes or until mixture begins to boil. Remove bay leaf. Garnish each serving with a piece of celery stalk.

PASTA, RICE, AND GRAINS

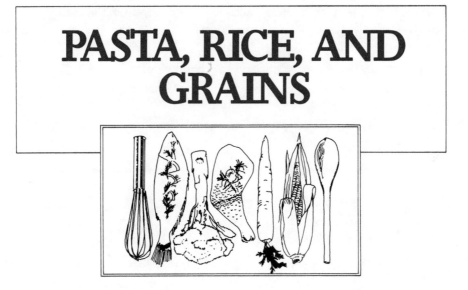

Light Fluffy Grains Produced in Microwave

• Do not expect to save time cooking grains in the microwave. Because of the volume of water needed, the cooking time is about the same as on a conventional stove.

• Do expect lighter, fluffier finished grains, minimal cleanup and energy-savings from your microwave oven.

• Do not expect to save time cooking pasta from scratch in the microwave. Because it, too, requires boiling a sizable amount of water, the cooking time is nearly the same as on a conventional stove.

Plain Pasta

For best results, microwave 6 ounces of spaghetti (or noodles or macaroni) in 4 quarts of water on High for 10–12 minutes. Drain it, then rinse it
to get rid of the starchy flavor. Mix desired Sauce (Spaghetti, Cheese,
Cream, etc.) into it and microwave on High for 10 more minutes, or until
heated through.

Macaroni and Cheese

Preparation Time: 40 minutes   *6 servings*

Pour into a 4-quart microwave-safe casserole:
    4 cups water
Cover and cook on High for 8–12 minutes, or until boiling.
Stir in:
    2 cups macaroni noodles, uncooked
Cover and cook on High for 2–4 minutes, or until boiling. Stir. Cook on
High another 2–4 minutes. Let stand 2–3 minutes, then rinse to get rid of
starchy flavor, and drain.
Pour Cheese Sauce (see page 27) over cooked macaroni, then microwave
on High for 5 more minutes, or until macaroni are heated through. Set
aside. Microwave on High for 45 seconds:
    2 tablespoons butter
Stir in:
    ¼ cup fine bread crumbs
Sprinkle over macaroni and serve.

Fettucine Alfredo

Preparation Time: 20 minutes   *4–6 servings*

Combine in 2-quart glass measure:
> **8 ounces dry fettucine**
> **4 cups water**
> **1 teaspoon oil**

Microwave on High for 10–12 minutes or until noodles are tender. Rinse with cold water and drain. Gently stir in:
> **1 cup half and half or light cream**
> **½ cup parmesan cheese**
> **1 teaspoon basil**
> **½ teaspoon salt**
> **⅛ teaspoon pepper**

Microwave on High for 4–6 minutes or until heated through.

Note: There are excellent sauce mixes available for microwave use that include all the dry ingredients and require only the addition of milk and butter.

Pasta Primavera

Preparation Time: 40–45 minutes   *6–8 servings*

Combine in 2-quart glass measure:
> **8 ounces dry fettucine**
> **4 cups water**
> **1 teaspoon oil**

Microwave on High for 10–12 minutes or until noodles are tender. Rinse with cold water and drain.
Combine in 3-quart covered casserole:
> **2 cups broccoli, cut up**
> **2 cups cauliflower, cut up**
> **1 cup carrots, thinly sliced**
> **1 medium zucchini, sliced**
> **1 clove garlic, minced**
> **2 tablespoons water**

Microwave on High for 11–13 minutes or until vegetables are tender. Drain and add to pasta, along with:
> **10–12 cherry tomatoes**
> **1 cup half and half or light cream**
> **½ cup parmesan cheese**

1 teaspoon basil
½ teaspoon salt
⅛ teaspoon pepper
Microwave on High for 6–8 minutes or until heated through.

Tuna Noodle Casserole

Preparation Time: 25 minutes   *4–6 servings*

Combine in 2-quart casserole:
1 cup water
1½ cups egg noodles, uncooked
Microwave on High for 5 minutes. Stir, then microwave again on high for 5 minutes. Stir in:
6-ounce can tuna
1 can cream of mushroom soup
¼ cup mushrooms (4 ounces)
2 cups peas (10-ounce package)
Cover with casserole lid. Microwave on High for 5 minutes. Top with:
crushed potato chips or butter crackers
Microwave on High for 4–6 minutes, uncovered.

Long-Grain Rice

Preparation Time: 20 minutes   *4–6 servings*

Combine in a 2-quart covered casserole:
1 cup rice
2 cups liquid (water or broth)
1 teaspoon salt
1 tablespoon butter
Microwave on High for 5 minutes or until mixture is boiling, then at 50% for 15 minutes or until rice is tender and liquid is absorbed.

Brown Rice

Preparation Time: 1¼ hours   4–6 servings

Combine in covered 2-quart casserole:
> **1 cup brown rice**
> **2½ cups chicken broth**
> **¼ cup water**
> **1 tablespoon instant onion**
> **⅛ teaspoon ground oregano**

Microwave on High for 8–10 minutes or until mixture is boiling, then at 50% for 45–60 minutes.

Micro-Fried Rice

Preparation Time: 10 minutes   4 servings

Combine in 1-quart microwave-safe casserole:
> **1 cup rice, cooked**
> **2 teaspoons soy sauce**
> **3 green onions, sliced**
> **1 teaspoon parsley flakes**
> **3 eggs, beaten**
> **½ cup water chestnuts, chopped**

Microwave covered on High for 3–5 minutes or until eggs are set. Stir before serving.

Spanish Rice

Preparation Time: 45 minutes   6 servings

Place in 1½-quart casserole, cover with paper towel, and microwave on High for 3–4 minutes or until crisp:
> **4 slices bacon**

Remove bacon and add to bacon drippings:
> **⅓ cup onion, chopped**
> **⅓ cup green pepper, chopped**

Microwave on High for 3–4 minutes, then stir in:
> **2 cups tomatoes, cut up**
> **¼ teaspoon celery salt**

Cover and microwave on High for 3–4 minutes, then stir in until moistened:
> **½ cup long grain rice**

Microwave on High for 25–30 minutes or until rice is tender. Sprinkle with crumbled bacon and:

½ cup cheddar cheese, shredded

Microwave on High for 1 minute, or until cheese is melted.

Oatmeal

Preparation Time: 5 minutes   *1 serving*

Stir together, then microwave on High for 1½ minutes:

¼ cup quick oats
½ cup water
pinch of salt

Stir, then cover and let stand 2–3 minutes. Serve, topped with fruit or brown sugar, and milk.

Big-Batch Oatmeal

Preparation Time: 10 minutes   *6 servings*

Stir together, then microwave on High for 4 minutes:

1½ cups oatmeal
3 cups water
¾ teaspoon salt

Stir, then cover and let stand 5 minutes. Serve, topped with fruit or brown sugar, and milk.

BEEF

Microwaved Meats are Flavorful

- Meats should be completely defrosted before cooking.
- Whenever possible, defrost in original wrappings, removing any ties, rings, foil, or wires.
- Place package of unwrapped meat in a microwave-safe dish.
- Defrost on Low only until meat becomes pliable. Remove from oven and allow standing time to complete the process.
- Meats cooked for more than 10 minutes will brown naturally. The more fat on the surface of the meat, the browner the finished product.
- The browning process can be enhanced by using browning agents, steak sauce, soy sauce, or spices, such as chili powder, pepper, or paprika.

Steak

Preparation Time: 10–15 minutes

For crisp surface :
Use browning dish. Preheat 2–10 minutes depending on size of browner and manufacturer's directions. Grease with butter or margarine for better color. Depending on size of piece of meat, microwave on High for 2–5 minutes on each side.

Preparation Time: 5–10 minutes

For moister, more tender surface :
Coat with favorite browning agent or seasoning (avoid salt). Place on meat rack. Cover with waxed paper. Microwave on High for 2–4 minutes per piece. Turn over and repeat process.

Beef Roast

Place roast on roasting rack, fat side down.
Coat with browning agent, if desired.
Insert probe, being careful to avoid bone, fat, or air pockets.
Cover tightly with lid or plastic wrap, or place in cooking bag.
Shield with foil areas that have a tendency to brown too quickly.
Turn large pieces of meat over halfway through cooking process to insure consistent doneness.
Roast at 30–70% to desired internal temperature, testing at several places to be sure the correct temperature has been reached throughout:

    Beef rare   120°F
    Beef medium   135°F
    Beef well done 160°F

Allow to stand 10 minutes.
Salt after cooking so the meat retains its moisture.
Carve and serve.

Chuck (or Less Tender) Roast

Preparation Time: 1–1¼ hours   *6–8 servings*

Coat nylon cooking bag with:
> **1 tablespoon flour**

Add:
> **3-pound roast, fat side down**
> **3–6 red potatoes, peeled**
> **3–6 carrots, peeled and pared**
> **6-ounce can tomato sauce**
> **6-ounces cooking wine**

Insert probe in the center of the muscle.
Seal bag with nylon tie. Microwave on High for 10 minutes.
Turn over. Insert probe and cook at 50% to 135°F.
Allow to stand 10 minutes.

Night-Before Pot Roast

Preparation Time: 40 minutes   *6 servings*

Combine in 9 × 13 glass baking dish:
> **1 package onion soup mix**
> **1 cup cooking wine**
> **½ teaspoon salt**
> **¼ teaspoon pepper**
> **2–3 pound chuck roast**

Cover with plastic wrap and refrigerate overnight. Turn over in the morning. Add:
> **4 small potatoes**
> **4 carrots, peeled and quarted**

Microwave at 50% for 35 minutes, or to 150°F.

Beef Cubes

Preparation Time: 1½–2 hours   *6 servings*

Combine in covered 3-quart casserole:

> **2 pounds beef cubes**
> **1 can beef broth (or 2 cups water and 2 bouillon cubes)**
> **1 medium onion, chopped**
> **¼ teaspoon pepper**

Microwave on High for 10 minutes, then at 30% for 90–100 minutes, or until tender.

Beef Burgundy

Preparation Time: 26 minutes   *4 servings*

Combine in 2-quart casserole:

> **2 medium carrots, peeled and cut into 1-inch pieces**
> **2 cups beef cubes, cooked**
> **1 cup cooking juices or beef broth**
> **½ cup fresh mushrooms**
> **1 cup whole onions**
> **1 clove garlic, minced**
> **1 bay leaf**
> **3 tablespoons red cooking wine**
> **1 teaspoon parsley flakes**
> **1 tablespoon flour**

Microwave on High for 15–17 minutes, stirring once or twice, or until carrots are tender.

Beef Stroganoff

Preparation Time: 12 minutes   *4 servings*

Combine in 1½-quart covered casserole:
> **2 cups beef cubes, cooked**
> **1 cup cooking juices or broth**
> **½ cup mushrooms, sliced**

Microwave on High for 5–6 minutes, or until mushrooms are tender.
Mix together and add to meat:
> **1 cup sour cream**
> **2 tablespoons flour**

Microwave on High for 2 minutes. Stir. Microwave on High another 2
minutes. Stir until thickened. Serve over buttered noodles.

Cheesy Meat Loaf

Preparation time: 12 minutes   *4 servings*

Combine in mixing bowl:
> **1 pound ground beef**
> **3 slices bread, moistened and crumbled**
> **1 egg**
> **1 small onion, chopped**
> **¼ cup catsup**
> **1 tablespoon worcestershire sauce**

Pat into baking ring and top with:
> **¼ cup parmesan cheese**

Cover with waxed paper. Microwave on High for 6–8 minutes.

Meat Loaf

Preparation time: 15 minutes   *6 servings*

Combine in mixing bowl:
> **1 pound ground beef**
> **½ pound ground pork**
> **1 envelope onion soup mix**
> **1 slice bread, crumbled**
> **1 egg**
> **¼ cup tomato juice or milk**

Pat into baking ring. Sprinkle with browning powder or reserved onion soup mix. Cover with waxed paper. Microwave on High for 6–8 minutes or to 150°F.

Defrosting and Cooking Ground Beef

• Defrost at 30% for 4 minutes per pound. Then allow 5 minutes standing time per pound to complete the defrosting process.

• To cook thoroughly, microwave on High for 5–6 minutes per pound.

• To eliminate excess fat, cook ground beef in a microwave-safe colander set in a casserole dish or pie plate to catch the drippings.

• Stir ground beef once or twice during cooking time to break up the lumps of meat.

• To enhance the cooked meat's color, sprinkle it with a browning agent or seasoning mix before microwaving.

• For even cooking, bake meat loaf in a ring pan or in a casserole dish with a glass tumbler inverted in the center.

• For even cooking, arrange meat balls in a circle on a plate or in a casserole dish.

• Because microwave ovens can make cooking such a speedy process, we offer here recipes that capitalize on that efficiency. Packaged sauces and mixes contribute to quickly preparing food. On the other hand, "from-scratch" chili and slowly stewed spaghetti sauce can also be made in the microwave. They may take as long as they do on a conventional stove, but cooking them in the microwave is still an efficient method, cleanup-wise.

To Prepare a Packaged Ground Beef Mix:

Crumble into casserole:
> **1 pound ground beef**

Microwave on High for 5–6 minutes. Drain fat and stir in:
> **1 package hamburger mix (7½ ounces)**
> **3¼ cups water**

Cover and microwave on High for 12–13 minutes, or until noodles are tender.

Cranberry Glazed Loaves

Preparation Time: 22 minutes   *4–6 servings*

Combine in mixing bowl:
> **1 egg, beaten**
> **⅓ cup milk**
> **⅓ cup quick cooking oats**
> **2 tablespoons onion, finely chopped**
> **½ teaspoon salt**
> **dash pepper**
> **1 pound ground beef**

Shape into 4 or 5 loaves. Place in a 9 × 13 baking pan and top with a combination of:
> **1 cup whole cranberry sauce**
> **1 cup brown sugar**
> **2 teaspoons lemon juice**

Arrange loaves in a circle and microwave at 80% for 12–15 minutes.

Chili

Preparation time: 20 minutes   *6 servings*

Crumble in 3-quart casserole:
> **1 pound ground beef**

Sprinkle with:
> **1½ teaspoons chili powder**
> **1½ teaspoons salt**
> **1 tablespoon flour**
> **1 onion, chopped fine**

Or:
> **1 envelope chili seasoning mix**

Microwave on High for 5 minutes. Stir in:
> **2 cups tomato sauce**
> **2 cups kidney beans, prepared**

Cover with casserole lid and cook on High for 6–8 minutes or until the chili reaches an internal temperature of 135°F.

Meat Balls and Tomato Sauce

Preparation time: 15 minutes   6 servings

Combine:
>**1 pound ground beef**
>**2 slices bread, torn into crumbs**
>**1 egg**
>**2 tablespoons oregano**
>**salt and pepper**

Shape into meat balls and arrange in single layer in 3-quart casserole.
Cover and microwave on High for 4 minutes. Pour over meatballs:
>**1 jar spaghetti sauce or 3 cups Home-Prepared Spaghetti**
>**Sauce (page 88)**

Cover. Microwave on High for 6–8 minutes or until heated through.

Lasagna

Preparation time: 1¼ hours   10 servings

Nothing needs to be precooked to make microwaved Lasagna. You will
not save much time but you will avoid a lot of mess. This dish works well
when you have time to prepare it ahead of time or want to have some-
thing time-cooked while you are away.
Divide the following ingredients into 3 layers in a 9 × 13-inch baking pan:
Layer 1:
>**9 lasagna noodles (use 3 noodles for each layer)**

Layer 2:
>**2 cups ricotta cheese (use ⅔ cup for each layer)**
>**1⅓ cups parmesan cheese (use ⅓ cup for each layer, reserv-**
>**ing ⅓ cup for top of finished casserole)**
>**1 cup mozzarella cheese, shredded (use ⅓ cup for each**
>**layer)**

Layer 3:
>**1 pound ground beef (use ⅓ cup for each layer)**
>**1 28-ounce or 35-ounce jar of spaghetti sauce or Home-**
>**Prepared Sauce, page 88 (use ¾–1 cup for each layer)**

Assemble layers, ending with spaghetti sauce. Cover with waxed paper.
Microwave on High for 10 minutes. Simmer at 50% for 30 minutes or to
an internal temperature of 150°F. Top with reserved cheese. Microwave on
High for 3–5 minutes.

Hamburgers

Form 1 pound of ground beef into 4 patties, adding chopped onion, seasoning, egg, tomato juice, and bread crumbs, if desired.

To microwave burgers on a paper-lined **plate** or **roasting rack**, cover with waxed paper, then microwave on High for 2 minutes to attain medium-rare burgers (microwave on High for 2½ minutes for medium-well-done burgers). Turn burgers over and cover. Microwave on High for 1–2 more minutes for medium-rare burgers (microwave on High for 2–3 minutes for medium-well-done burgers).

Allow to stand, covered, for 1–2 minutes to complete cooking and to attain a browner color.

To microwave burgers on a **browning dish**, preheat dish according to manufacturer's directions. Microwave on High for 2 minutes to attain medium rare burgers (microwave on High for 2½ minutes for medium-well-done burgers).

Turn burgers over and microwave on High for 1–2 more minutes for medium-rare burgers (microwave on High for 2–3 minutes for medium-well-done burgers).

Burgers may be eaten immediately since standing time is not needed.

Hamburger-Stuffed Squash

Preparation Time: 40 minutes   *6 servings*

Place in microwave oven:
>   **2 whole acorn squash, pierced**

Microwave on High for 10 minutes. Rearrange, then microwave at 50% for 5–7 minutes. Combine in 2-quart casserole:
>   **¾ pound ground beef**
>   **¾ cup celery, chopped**
>   **3 tablespoons onion, chopped**

Microwave on High for 4–6 minutes.
Stir in:
>   **1 medium cooking apple, peeled, cored, and chopped**
>   **(1 cup)**

Microwave on High for 45 seconds. Drain fat.
Combine and stir into beef mixture:
>   **1 egg, slightly beaten**
>   **½ cup dairy sour cream**

Cut squash in half; scoop out seeds; place cut side up and fill squash halves with beef mixture. Microwave on High for 5 minutes. Sprinkle with:

¾ cup mild cheese, grated

Microwave at 50% for 1 minute to melt cheese. Serve hot.

Apple Ground Beef Stuffing

Preparation time: 18 minutes   *4–6 servings*

Combine in 3-quart casserole:

1 pound ground beef
¼ cup onion, chopped
¼ cup celery, chopped
1 apple, pared and chopped

Microwave on High for 5–6 minutes or until vegetables are tender and beef is cooked.
Stir in:

1 cup water or apple juice

Microwave on High for 2 minutes or until juice is boiling. Stir in:

2 cups seasoned stuffing mix

Cover and let stand 5 minutes or until moisture is absorbed. Fluff with a fork.

Ground Beef and Rice

Preparation Time: 23 minutes   *6 servings*

Microwave in 2-quart casserole for 5-minutes:

1 pound ground beef
1 small onion, chopped
¼ cup green pepper, chopped

Drain fat. Break up meat and stir in:

1 cup rice or macaroni, uncooked
2 cups spaghetti sauce (see page 88)
1 cup water
1 cup cheese, grated

Cover with casserole lid and microwave on High to 150°F, about 12 minutes. Stir and microwave on High for 8–10 minutes longer. You may need to add more water if rice begins to dry out before becoming tender.

Chinese Casserole

Combine in 1½-quart casserole:
> **1 can chicken noodle soup**
> **1 can water**
> **¾ cup quick cooking rice**

Microwave 3–4 minutes. Let stand, covered.
Cook in 2-quart casserole on High for 5–6 minutes:
> **1 pound ground beef**
> **1 large onion, sliced**
> **½ cup green pepper, chopped**
> **½ cup celery, chopped**

Drain and stir in rice mixture. Cover and microwave on High for 3–4 minutes.

Hearty Onion Bake

Preparation Time: 20 minutes   *6 servings*

Microwave on High for 4–6 minutes:
> **½ pound pork sausage, removed from casing**
> **½ pound ground beef**

Drain fat and divide between 6 1-cup casseroles.
Combine and divide between casseroles:
> **1 envelope onion soup mix**
> **1½ cups milk**
> **2 eggs, beaten**

Microwave on High for 2–4 minutes.
Top with:
> **6 slices melba rounds**
> **6 slices tomato**
> **¼ cup mild cheese, shredded**

Microwave on High for 2–4 minutes to melt cheese. Serve warm.

Cabbage Rolls

Preparation time: 35 minutes   *6 servings*

In 2-quart glass measure microwave on High for 5–6 minutes or until boiling:

2 cups water

Immerse into boiling water:

12 cabbage leaves, open side up, stem side down

Cover with plastic wrap and microwave on High for 5 minutes. Let stand while mixing filling.

Combine:

1 pound ground beef
2 potatoes, shredded
1 medium onion, chopped
½ cup celery, chopped
1 teaspoon salt
1 teaspoon instant beef bouillon
1 teaspoon mustard
1 teaspoon worcestershire sauce
⅛ teaspoon pepper
1 egg

Drain cabbage leaves. Place ⅓ cup meat filling at thin edge of leaf. Fold in sides. Roll with filling inside. Place in glass baking dish with:

¼ cup water

Cover with plastic wrap. Microwave on High for 12–13 minutes.

Serve with tomato sauce or Seasoned White Sauce.

Seasoned White Sauce

Use Basic White Sauce (page 27) and stir in:

⅓ cup sour cream
1 teaspoon chives

Top with paprika.

Creamed Dried Beef

Preparation Time: 10 minutes   *4–6 servings*

Combine in 1½-quart casserole:
> **2 tablespoons margarine**
> **4 ounces dried beef, shredded**

Microwave on High for 2 minutes. Stir in:
> **2 tablespoons flour**

Microwave on High for 1 minute and gradually stir in:
> **1 cup warm milk**

Microwave on High for 2 minutes. Stir. Microwave on High another 2 minutes.

Note: More cooking time may be necessary for a thicker sauce.

Home-Prepared Spaghetti Sauce

Preparation Time: 10 minutes   *Yields 4 cups*

Microwave on High for 6–8 minutes or until internal temperature of 150°F is reached:
> **1 cup onion, chopped**
> **3 cups pureed tomatoes**
> **1 6-ounce can tomato paste**
> **1 teaspoon basil**
> **1 tablespoon oregano**
> **1 teaspoon salt**
> **¼ teaspoon pepper**

PORK

Please see page 76 for guidelines on defrosting and cooking meats in the microwave.

Pork Roast

Place roast on roasting rack, fat side down.
Coat with browning agent, if desired.
Insert probe, being careful to avoid bone, fat, or air pockets.
Cover tightly with lid or plastic wrap, or place in cooking bag.
Shield with foil areas that have a tendency to brown too quickly.
Turn large pieces of meat over halfway through cooking process to insure consistent doneness.
Roast at 30–70% to 160°F , testing at several places to be sure the correct temperature has been reached throughout.
Allow to stand 10 minutes.
Salt after cooking so the meat retains its moisture.
Carve and serve.

Pork Chops

Preparation Time: 10–15 minutes

For crisp cuts:
Use browning dish. Preheat 2–10 minutes depending on size of browner and manufacturer's directions. Grease with butter or margarine for better color. Depending on size of piece of meat, microwave on High for 2–5 minutes on each side.

Preparation Time: 5–10 minutes

For moister, more tender cuts:
Coat with favorite browning agent or seasoning (avoid salt). Place on meat rack. Cover with waxed paper. Microwave on High for 2–4 minutes per piece. Turn over and repeat process.

Fully Cooked Ham

Preparation Time: 5–8 minutes per pound
Most hams are fully cooked and only need to be warmed.

Place ham on roasting rack and cover to retain heat and moisture. Cook at 30–50% to an internal temperature of 120°–130°F.

Bacon

Place paper towel on roasting rack or paper plate. Arrange bacon in single layer. Cover with paper towel. Microwave on High for about 1 minute per slice or 15 minutes per pound.

Note: See page 197 for Bacon Appetizers.

Apple Stuffed Tenderloin

Preparation Time: 25 minutes   *4–6 servings*

Combine in microwave-safe bowl:

2 tablespoons butter
2 tablespoons celery, chopped
2 tablespoons onion, chopped

Microwave on High for 2 minutes or until vegetables are tender. Stir in:

1½ cups stuffing mix
½ cup hot water

Slice lengthwise, three-quarters of the way through, then flatten and pound to even thickness:

1½ pounds pork tenderloin

Fill with stuffing mixture and place on microwave roasting rack. Sprinkle with salt and pepper. Cover and microwave at 80% for 10 minutes. Combine and spoon over meat:

1 envelope brown gravy mix
¼ cup brown sugar
1 20-ounce can apple pie filling

Cover and microwave at 80% for 4–6 minutes longer, or until meat reaches an internal temperature of 160° F.

Pork and Rice a L'orange

Preparation Time: 20 minutes   *4 servings*

Combine in 1½-quart glass baking dish:

½ cup minute rice
½ cup orange juice
2 tablespoons raisins
1 tablespoon water
2 teaspoons brown sugar
¼ teaspoon salt
⅛ teaspoon ground cinnamon

Mix well. Then arrange on top of rice mixture:

> **1 pork tenderloin cut into 1-inch slices and seasoned with salt, pepper, and paprika**

Cover with waxed paper and microwave on High for 9–10 minutes, or until rice is tender and cutlets are done.

Pork Chop-Noodle Dinner

Combine in glass baking dish:

> **2 cups narrow noodles**
> **1 small onion, chopped**
> **1¼ cups water**
> **⅓ cup catsup**
> **½ teaspoon salt**
> **⅛ teaspoon pepper**

Arrange on top of noodles

> **2 pounds pork chops**

Top with browning powder or paprika. Microwave on High for 22–25 minutes or until tender.

Barbecued Ribs

Preparation Time: 30 minutes   *4 servings*

Arrange in glass baking dish:

> **2 pounds country-style ribs**

Cover with waxed paper and microwave on High for 7 minutes. Turn over and microwave on High another 7 minutes.
Combine and brush onto ribs:

> **1 cup catsup**
> **⅓ cup frozen concentrated lemonade**
> **3 tablespoons brown sugar**
> **2 tablespoons onion, chopped**
> **¼ teaspoon celery seed**

Microwave on High for 11–12 minutes, or until tender. The ribs can also be roasted over hot coals at this point.

Sweet and Sour Pork Kabobs

Preparation time: 25 minutes   *4−6 servings*

Combine in covered 1-quart casserole:
> **6 carrots, peeled and cut into 1-inch pieces**
> **2 tablespoons soy sauce**

Microwave on High for 3−3½ minutes, or until steaming hot.
Add:
> **1 pound boneless pork, cut into 1-inch cubes**

Cover. Microwave on High for 6−7 minutes. Set aside.
Combine in 2-cup microwave-safe measure:
> **juice from 8-ounce can of pineapple chunks**
> **2 tablespoons sugar**
> **2 teaspoons cornstarch**
> **1 tablespoon soy sauce**
> **1 tablespoon vinegar**
> **1 tablespoon sweet pickle relish**

Mix until smooth. Microwave uncovered on High for 3−4 minutes or until mixture boils and thickens, stirring twice.
Prepare:
> **1 green pepper, cut into 1-inch pieces**

Thread carrots, pineapple chunks, green pepper, and pork alternately on 6-inch bamboo skewers. Arrange on microwave-safe platter and brush with sweet and sour sauce. Cover with waxed paper. Microwave on High for 3−4 minutes.

Orange-Glazed Ham Slices

Preparation time: 11 minutes   *5 servings*

Arrange on microwave-safe meat rack:
> **5 slices ham, about 1 pound**

Cover with waxed paper. Microwave at 80% for 4−5 minutes. Set aside.
Combine in microwave-safe 1-cup measure:
> **2 tablespoons orange marmalade**
> **1 tablespoon dijon-style mustard**
> **⅛ teaspoon paprika**

Microwave on High for 30−40 seconds or until mixture bubbles. Spoon over ham slices. Garnish with orange slices and parsley.

Pork Cassoulet

Preparation Time: 18 minutes   *6–8 servings*

Combine in microwaveable colander combination or 2-quart casserole:

½ pound pork sausage, removed from casing
1 small onion, sliced
1 clove garlic, minced

Microwave on High for 2–4 minutes or until browned.
Turn into 2-quart casserole:

2 15-ounce cans navy beans with juice
1½ cups fully cooked ham, cubed
¼ cup dry white cooking wine, optional
2 tablespoons parsley, snipped
1 bay leaf
dash of ground cloves

Microwave on High for 10–12 minutes, stirring occasionally. Remove bay leaf. Serve in bowls.

Ham and Cheese Casserole

Preparation Time: 20 minutes   *6–8 servings*

Combine in 3-quart casserole dish:

8-ounce package noodles, cooked
2 cups fully cooked ham, cut in pieces
1 ½ cups cheese, shredded
1 can cream of mushroom soup
1 cup frozen peas
½ teaspoon dry mustard

Top with:

1 can fried onion rings

Cover with casserole lid and microwave at 80% for 12–15 minutes.

Sausage and Apple Rings

Place in 1-quart glass baking dish:
> **2 medium apples, cored and sliced in ½ inch slices**
> **1 cup cranberry juice cocktail**

Microwave on High for 4–6 minutes.
Combine while apples are cooking:
> **1 tablespoon cornstarch**
> **2 teaspoons sugar**
> **2 teaspoons water**

Remove apples from juice and stir in cornstarch mixture. Stir, then microwave on High for 3–4 minutes or until sauce thickens. Set aside.
Shape into 4 patties:
> **1 pound apple sausage**

Dip into:
> **1 egg, beaten**

Then dip into:
> **¾ cup cracker crumbs, finely ground (about 20 saltines)**

Brown on browning dish for 5–8 minutes.
Top patties with apple slices and thickened sauce.

Sausage-Macaroni Skillet

Preparation Time: 25 minutes   *6–8 servings*

Combine in microwave-safe colander combination and microwave on High for 4–6 minutes:
> **1 pound italian sausage, removed from casing**
> **½ cup green peppers, chopped**
> **½ cup onion, chopped**

Combine sausage mixture in 3-quart casserole with:
> **16-ounce can tomatoes, cut up**
> **10-ounce can pizza sauce**
> **¼ teaspoon salt**

Microwave on High for 4–6 minutes. Stir in:
> **2 cups zucchini, thinly sliced**

Microwave on High for 2–3 minutes or until zucchini is tender. Stir in:
> **1 cup medium-sized shell macaroni, cooked**

Sprinkle with:
> **1 cup mozzarella cheese, shredded**

Microwave on High for 2–3 minutes until cheese is melted and macaroni is warm.

Rice and Sausage Casserole

Preparation Time: 20 minutes   6 servings

Microwave on High for 4–6 minutes in microwaveable colander combination or 2-quart casserole:
>**1 pound pork sausage, removed from casing**
>**1 small onion, finely chopped**

Drain fat and layer in 2-quart casserole with sausage mixture:
>**3 cups rice, cooked**

Pour on:
>**1 can condensed tomato, celery, mushroom or chicken soup**

Sprinkle over top:
>**¼ cup cheddar cheese, shredded**

Cover and microwave on High 6–8 minutes.

Night-Before Sausage Brunch

Preparation Time: 35 minutes   6–8 servings

Layer in 9 × 13 greased microwave-safe baking dish:
>**12 link sausages, cooked**
>**12 slices bread, buttered and cubed**
>**1 cup cheese, shredded**

Mix and pour over bread and sausage:
>**8 eggs**
>**4 cups milk**

Cover with a thick layer of:
>**cornflake crumbs, crushed**

Cover, refrigerate overnight, then microwave at 50% for 25–35 minutes or until set in the center.

Sausage Panwiches

Spread **2 tablespoons applebutter** on **2 cooked pancakes.** Set aside. Crumble into 1-quart glass microwave-safe dish:
>**¼ cup loose sausage, cooked or 1 link pre-cooked sausage**

Microwave on High for 2 minutes. Sprinkle over pancakes. Microwave on High for 30–45 seconds.

Hot Dogs

Place regular-sized **hot dog** in bun. Wrap in paper towel and microwave on High for 30–50 seconds.

Stuffed Hot Dogs

Preparation time: 10 minutes   4 servings

Microwave between paper towels on High for 2–3 minutes:
> **4 slices bacon**

Slit:
> **4 hot dogs**

Stuff with:
> **4 slices cheese**
> **mustard**
> **relish**

Wrap with partially cooked bacon. Secure with wooden picks. Microwave between paper towels on High for 2–3 minutes. Remove wooden picks and serve in warm rolls.

Hot Dogs and Sauerkraut

Preparation Time: 15 minutes   8 servings

Combine in 2-quart casserole:
> **1 package brown gravy mix**
> **¼ cup brown sugar**
> **½ cup beer or apple juice**
> **1 pound sauerkraut**
> **1 small onion, sliced**

Mix in:
> **1 pound hot dogs, scored**

Cover with lid. Microwave on High for 8–10 minutes or to 135°F.
Note: Wursts or other meats can be substituted for hot dogs.

Hot Dogs and Baked Beans

Arrange **4 hot dogs** in casserole. Cover with **16-ounce can of baked beans.** Microwave at 80% for 6–8 minutes.

POULTRY

Quick Cooking Creates Moist, Tender Meat

• Defrost at 30% for 7–8 minutes per pound. Make sure meat is completely defrosted before beginning to cook it.

• Whenever possible remove the skin from the bird before microwaving it. Because of its high fat content the skin retains moisture and, thus, never gets crisp and even prevents proper cooking of the meat itself.

• Cover the bird to retain moisture while cooking. The tighter the cover, the more moist the meat. Plastic wrap, a cooking bag, or a tightly fitting casserole lid all work well.

• Microwave poultry on a rack to elevate it above its hot juices, which may overcook its underside.

• Microwave at 70% for 7½ minutes per pound. Whole poultry up to 14 pounds can be microwaved.

• Stuffing does not increase the per-pound cooking time.

• Use aluminum foil to cover portions that may seem to be cooking too quickly, like the wings or drumsticks.

• Turn bird over halfway through cooking time.

• Be sure there is enough room around the bird in your oven—at least one inch on all sides—to allow for the proper circulation of air and microwaves.

• Standing time is essential to assure that the roast bird is fully cooked. Allow 7–10 minutes.

Chicken Breasts

For maximum crispness remove skin and coat with Crisp Crumb Mixture (below).
Arrange on roasting rack, with the thickest part of the meat toward the outside.
Cover with waxed paper or plastic wrap.
Microwave at 70% for 7½ minutes per pound (whole breasts weigh close to a pound).

Chicken Pieces

Coat with Crisp Crumb Mixture or chicken-coating mix.
Arrange on meat rack with thicker portions to the outside.
Cover with plastic wrap or waxed paper.
Microwave at 70% for 7½ minutes per pound.

Crisp Crumb Mixture

Combine:

> **½ cup dry bread crumbs**
> **½ cup parmesan cheese**
> **½ teaspoon paprika**
> **dash pepper**

Soy Chicken

Preparation Time: 25 minutes   *6–8 servings*

Place in cooking bag, then set in glass baking dish:

> **2½-pound chicken, stuffed with**
> **1 small onion**

Combine and pour over chicken:

> **¼ cup soy sauce**
> **¼ cup orange juice**
> **¼ teaspoon ground ginger**

Seal bag. Pierce. Microwave at 70% for 18–20 minutes.

Barbecued Chicken

Microwave chicken pieces at 70% for 3½ minutes per pound.
Brush with Barbecue Sauce (below).
Turn pieces over and brush with Sauce.
Microwave at 70% for another 3½ minutes per pound or roast over
hot coals.

Barbecue Sauce

Combine and mix well:
> **1 cup catsup**
> **⅓ cup frozen concentrated lemonade**
> **3 tablespoons brown sugar**
> **2 tablespoons onion, chopped**
> **¼ teaspoon celery seed**

Sweet and Sour Chicken

Preparation Time: 20 minutes   *4 servings*

Combine in pie plate:
> **3 tablespoons flour**
> **½ cup brown sugar**
> **¼ teaspoon salt**

Cut into ½-inch cubes:
> **1½ pounds chicken**

Coat with flour mixture and arrange in baking pan. Combine and pour
over chicken:
> **¼ cup soy sauce**
> **⅓ cup vinegar**
> **¼ cup water**

Top with:
> **1 onion, sliced**
> **1 pepper, sliced**

Microwave on High for 6 minutes. Stir. Microwave on High for 6 more
minutes.

Chicken Parmesan

Preparation Time: 20 minutes   *4 servings*

Combine in pie plate:
>**2 tablespoons flour**
>**½ teaspoon salt**
>**dash pepper**

Dredge in flour mixture:
>**2 boneless chicken breasts**

Dip in egg wash mixture of:
>**1 egg**
>**2 tablespoons milk or water**

Dip in:
>**Crisp Crumb Mixture (page 101)**

Brown in browning dish.
Layer in small casserole dish:
>**½ cup spaghetti sauce (see page 88)**
>**breaded and browned chicken breasts**
>**¼ cup parmesan cheese**
>**¼ cup mozzarella cheese, grated**

Microwave on High for 4–6 minutes until cheese is melted and sauce is bubbling.

Chicken Kiev

Preparation Time: 25 minutes   *4 servings*

Pound until even thickness:
>**4 boneless chicken breasts**

Stuff each piece of chicken with:
>**4 tablespoons butter, frozen in 4 pats**
>**salt**
>**pepper**
>**chives**

Tuck in sides and roll.
Dip each roll in:
>**4 tablespoons butter, melted**

Roll in:
>**cracker crumbs, crushed** or **coating mix**

Position in baking pan on top of Stuffing (see page 55). Cover with waxed paper. Microwave at 80% for 15 minutes.

Cordon Bleu

Preparation Time: 25 minutes	4 servings

Pound until even thickness:

4 boneless chicken breasts

Layer on top of each piece of chicken:

4 slices cooked ham

4 slices gruyere cheese

Roll up each breast and dip in:

4 tablespoons butter, melted

Roll in:

cracker crumbs, crushed

Position in baking pan on top of Stuffing (see page 55). Cover with waxed paper. Microwave at 80% for 15 minutes.

Chicken and Rice

Preparation Time: 27 minutes	6 servings

Combine in 5-quart casserole or 9 × 13 glass dish:

1½ cups rice, uncooked

1 can cream of mushroom, celery, or chicken soup

4-ounce can mushrooms

1½ cups water

Top with:

3 pounds chicken pieces

Cover with lid or plastic wrap. Microwave on High for 10 minutes. Rotate pan. Microwave on High for 10–12 more minutes or until rice is tender and chicken is done.

Chicken-Rice Bake

Preparation Time: 35 minutes	*4–6 servings*

Place on paper plate between paper towels:
> **3 slices bacon**

Microwave on High for 3 minutes or until crisp.
Set aside.
Combine in 12 × 8 glass baking dish:
> **¾ cup rice**
> **1 cup chicken broth**
> **1 can condensed cream soup**

Cover with waxed paper. Microwave on High for 6–7 minutes. Stir in:
> **bacon, crumbled**

Top with:
> **2–3 pounds frying chicken, cut in pieces**

Sprinkle with browning powder or paprika. Microwave at 70% for 15 to 23 minutes.

Chicken a la King

Preparation Time: 12 minutes	*4–6 servings*

Combine in 1½-quart microwave-safe casserole:
> **2 tablespoons margarine**
> **4 ounces chicken, cubed and cooked**

Microwave on High for 2 minutes. Stir in:
> **2 tablespoons flour**

Microwave on High for 1 minute and gradually stir in:
> **1 cup warm milk**
> **½ cup mixed vegetables**

Microwave on High for 3 minutes. Stir, then serve in pastry shells or over rice.

Note: This is a handy way to use leftover chicken and vegetables.

VEAL

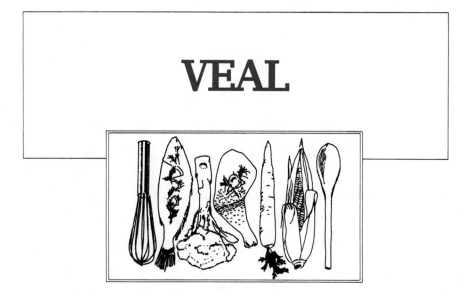

Please see page 76 for guidelines on defrosting and cooking meats in the microwave.

Veal Cutlets

Preparation Time: 20 minutes   *3–4 servings*

Combine in pie plate:
>**2 tablespoons flour**
>**½ teaspoon salt**
>**dash pepper**

Work flour mixture into:
>**2 veal cutlets**

Preheat Browning Dish and add:
>**4 tablespoons butter**
>**1 onion, sliced**

Add cutlets. Microwave on High for 3 minutes. Turn. Microwave on High another 3 minutes. Cover. Microwave at 30% for 2–3 more minutes, or until the meat is tender.

Veal Tenderloin

Preparation time: 15 minutes   *3–4 servings*

Combine in 1-cup microwave-safe measuring cup:
>**⅓ cup pineapple juice**
>**2 tablespoons brown sugar**
>**1 teaspoon cornstarch**
>**⅛ teaspoon dry mustard**
>**dash ground cloves**
>**⅛ teaspoon paprika**

Blend until smooth. Microwave uncovered on High for 1-1½ minutes or until mixture boils. Set aside.
Place in microwave-safe dish:
>**¾ pound veal tenderloin**

Brush with sauce. Cover. Cook at 80% for 8 minutes or until internal temperature reaches 130°F. Slice and serve with pineapples and remaining sauce.

Veal Scallopini

Preparation Time: 20 minutes   *4 servings*

Combine:
> **1 tablespoon flour**
> **½ teaspoon salt**
> **dash pepper**

Dredge in flour mixture:
> **1 pound veal, thinly sliced**

Microwave on High for 2 minutes to heat, then add meat to:
> **¼ cup salad oil**

Add:
> **½ onion, sliced**

Microwave on High for 4–6 minutes, or until tender, then add:
> **1 16-ounce can tomatoes, cut up and drained**
> **1 3-ounce can sliced mushrooms, drained**
> **1 tablespoon parsley, snipped**
> **¼ teaspoon garlic salt**
> **¼ teaspoon dried oregano**

Cook on High for 5–6 minutes or until heated through. Serve over hot buttered noodles.

Veal Scallops and Spaghetti

Preparation Time: 25 minutes   *3 servings*

Microwave 6 cups water on High for 10–12 minutes, or until boiling.
Add:

6 ounces spaghetti

Cover and microwave on High for 12–14 minutes.
Drain and rinse in cold water. Set aside.
Combine in 2-cup glass measure:

1 cup fresh mushrooms, sliced
1 small onion, sliced
1 clove garlic, minced
1 tablespoon margarine

Microwave uncovered on High for 3–4 minutes or until tender, stirring once.
Mix in:

½ teaspoon salt
¼ teaspoon oregano leaves
1 can (8 ounces) tomato sauce

Set aside.
Pound with meat mallet until very thin:

8 ounces veal scallops or cutlets

Sprinkle both sides with:

natural meat browning and seasoning powder

Cut into half-inch strips. Place in 1-quart glass casserole. Pour sauce over meat.
Microwave uncovered on High for 7–8 minutes or until veal is tender.
Place spaghetti on glass serving plate. Spoon meat sauce over spaghetti.
Microwave on High for 1½–2 minutes or until heated.

FISH AND SEAFOOD

Flavorful and Tender

• To defrost, place fish on a rack to allow its juices to drain. Then cover and microwave at 30% for 5–6 minutes per pound. (Fish should still be cold to the touch when defrosted.)

• To cook, place fish in baking pan with the thicker edges to the outside. Cover with plastic wrap or waxed paper. Microwave at 70% for 5–6 minutes per pound.

• Fish is done when its appearance changes from translucent to opaque or dull white. The meat will separate into flakes when touched with a fork.

• Fish blends well with many flavors. Experiment by sprinkling it lightly with freshly squeezed lemon juice, chopped fresh tomatoes, minced onion or garlic, fresh herbs or dried spices.

• Develop a crisp crust on breaded fish by using a browning dish (check manufacturer's directions) or by microwaving it in preheated oil.

• Shell fish are perfectly constructed for cooking in the microwave! They are individually encased in a natural cooking vessel and so are perfectly suited to waterless cooking.

• Place shellfish on paper plate and microwave at 70% until done;

• **Clams** are done when their shells open—about 2 minutes per dozen.

• **Crabs** are done when their shells turn pink. The cooking time varies considerably depending on the size of the crab, so watch carefully.

• **Lobster** is done when its shell turns red. That may take from 4 to 10 minutes, depending upon its size.

• **Oysters** are done when their shells open–about 2–5 minutes per dozen.

• **Shrimp** are done when their shells turn pink—about 1 minute per dozen, again, depending upon their size.

Fresh Catch

Preparation Time: 12 minutes   *4–6 servings*

Arrange in glass baking dish with thicker portions toward outside of dish:

2–3 small cleaned fish or 1-pound fillet
1 small onion, sliced
½ lemon, squeezed
salt and pepper

Cover with plastic wrap and microwave at 70% for 5–8 minutes or until fish looks opaque and flakes with a fork.

Fish in Wine Sauce

Preparation Time: 10 minutes   *4 servings*

Arrange in 8-inch square baking dish with thicker portions to the outside:

1 pound fish fillets

Cover with waxed paper. Microwave at 70% for 5–8 minutes or until fish is opaque and flakes.

Combine in 1-cup glass measure and microwave on High for 1 minute, then stir to combine:

1 tablespoon butter
2 tablespoons lemon juice
2 tablespoons cooking wine
½ teaspoon salt

Arrange fillets on serving dish. Drizzle with sauce and garnish with:

paprika, lemon slices, parsley

Fish Fillets with Mushrooms

Preparation Time: 10 minutes   *2–3 servings*

Arrange in 12 × 7 inch baking dish:

1 pound fish fillets

Combine and pour over fish:

1 teaspoon lemon juice
2 tablespoons water

Top with:

2 green onions, thinly sliced
½ cup mushrooms, sliced
1 tomato, peeled and cubed

Cover with waxed paper. Microwave at 70% for 5–7 minutes.

Yogurt Fillets

Preparation Time: 8 minutes   *About 4 servings*

Arrange in 8-inch round glass baking dish:

14–16 ounces haddock or other fish fillets

Cover with plastic wrap.

Microwave on High for 4–4½ minutes or until fish flakes apart easily with fork.

Combine for sauce:

⅓ cup plain yogurt
½ teaspoon salt
1 teaspoon mustard
1 teaspoon chopped pimento
1 teaspoon fresh parsley
1 teaspoon lemon juice

Drain fish. Spoon sauce over fish.

Microwave on High for 1–1½ minutes or until sauce is heated through.

Crunchy Fillets

Preparation Time: 7 minutes   *About 2 servings*

Place in shallow 1½-quart glass baking dish:

2 tablespoons butter or margarine

Microwave on High for ½–1 minute or until melted.

Arrange in butter:

8 ounces fish fillets

Turn to coat both sides.

Combine:

2 tablespoons almonds, finely chopped
2 tablespoons wheat germ
1 tablespoon parmesan cheese
¼ teaspoon salt

Spoon onto fillets. Cover with paper towel.

Microwave on High for 2½–3½ minutes or until fish flakes apart easily with fork.

Note: For a double recipe, increase final microwave time to 4–5 minutes. If desired, toast almonds before adding by placing in glass pie plate and microwaving on High for 4–5 minutes. Stir every minute.

Stuffed Trout

Preparation Time: 20 minutes   *3 servings*

Combine in glass mixing bowl:

> **3 tablespoons butter or margarine**
> **½ cup celery, chopped**
> **2 tablespoons onion, chopped**

Microwave uncovered on High for 4–4½ minutes or until vegetables are tender.

Stir in:

> **3 slices bread, cubed**
> **1 teaspoon dried parsley flakes**

Rinse and pat dry:

> **1 whole trout (about 16 ounces)**

Sprinkle cavity with:

> **½ teaspoon salt**

Place on glass serving plate. Spoon stuffing mixture into cavity, letting excess stuffing overflow.

Place on stuffing inside cavity:

> **2–3 slices lemon**

Cover with plastic wrap.

Microwave on High for 6–7 minutes or until fish flakes apart easily with fork, rotating plate once. Let stand covered a few minutes before serving. If desired, garnish with additional lemon slices and parsley.

Note: Stuffing can be prepared ahead and inserted just before cooking. Lemon slices can be omitted. Add 1 tablespoon lemon juice to stuffing.

Sole Florentine

Preparation Time: 20 minutes   *About 4 servings*

In microwave-safe container, microwave on High for 5–6 minutes or until thawed:

1 package (10 ounces) frozen chopped spinach

Drain. Arrange in 8-inch round glass baking dish.

Arrange on top of spinach:

12 ounces sole or other fish fillets

Set aside.

Combine:

1 cup milk
2 tablespoons flour
1 teaspoon salt
½ teaspoon tarragon leaves

Mix well.

Add:

2 tablespoons butter or margarine

Microwave uncovered on High for 3–4 minutes or until mixture boils and thickens, stirring twice during last half of cooking time.

Stir in:

1 tablespoon lemon juice

Pour over fillets.

Sprinkle with:

¼ cup parmesan cheese
paprika

Cover with waxed paper.

Microwave on High for 5–6 minutes or until fish flakes apart easily with fork, rotating dish once.

Note: The spinach can be thawed and sauce prepared several hours ahead. Assemble with fish just before cooking and serving.

Shrimp in a Dish

Preparation Time: 10 minutes   *4 servings*

Arrange in 9-inch glass pie plate:
> **1 pound shrimp, peeled**

Combine in glass measure and pour over shrimp:
> **2 tablespoons cooking sherry**
> **1 clove garlic, pressed**
> **dash red pepper sauce**
> **juice from ½ lemon**

Top shrimp with:
> **6 butter crackers, crushed into crisp crumbs**

Cover with waxed paper. Microwave on High for 4–6 minutes. Serve with lemon wedges.

Oriental Shrimp

Preparation Time: 20 minutes   *5–6 servings*

Combine in 1½-quart glass casserole:
> **¼ cup butter or margarine**
> **2 cups fresh mushrooms, sliced**
> **¼ cup green onions, sliced**
> **1 clove garlic, minced**

Microwave uncovered on High for 2–3 minutes, or until nearly tender.
Stir in:
> **1 tablespoon arrowroot or 2 tablespoons cornstarch**
> **2 tablespoons soy sauce**
> **½ teaspoon salt**
> **12 ounces frozen uncooked shrimp**

Cover with casserole lid.
Microwave on High for 5–6 minutes or until shrimp are no longer icy, stirring once.
Run warm water over, until separated:
> **1 package (6 ounces) frozen pea pods**

Stir in pea pods and:
> **1 cup fresh bean sprouts**

Cover.
Microwave on High for 6–7 minutes or vegetables are tender and shrimp are firm, stirring once or twice. Can be served alone or over rice.

Individual Salmon Loaves

Preparation Time: 25 minutes   4–5 servings

Combine in mixing bowl:
> **1 can (15½ ounces) salmon, drained**
> **1 egg**

Mix with fork.

Stir in:
> **1 cup soft bread crumbs**
> **⅓ cup milk**
> **2 tablespoons onion, finely chopped**
> **1 tablespoon lemon juice**
> **¼ teaspoon salt**
> **dash pepper**

Mix well. Spoon evenly into four or five 5-ounce glass custard cups and press firmly. Place cups on glass plate or tray for ease in transferring to oven. Cover with waxed paper.

Microwave on High for 5½–6 minutes or until centers of loaves are set, rotating plate once. Let stand covered and set aside.

Microwave in microwave-safe container on High for 5–6 minutes or until tender:
> **1 package (10 ounces) cut asparagus or spears**

Set aside.

Beat together with fork in 1-cup glass measure:
> **½ cup mayonnaise**
> **1 egg**

Mix in:
> **1 tablespoon lemon juice**
> **¼ teaspoon tarragon leaves**
> **¼ teaspoon prepared mustard**

Microwave uncovered at 50% for 1¼–1½ minutes, or until slightly thickened, stirring twice.

Unmold salmon onto serving plate. Arrange asparagus in center of or around salmon. Spoon sauce over salmon and asparagus.

Microwave uncovered on High for 1–2 minutes or until heated through.

Note: Salmon loaves can be made ahead and refrigerated 1–2 days. Increase first microwave time to 7–7½ minutes. If cooking only half the loaves, decrease time to 3–4 minutes.

Coquilles St. Jacques (*Scallops in Cream Sauce*)

Preparation Time: 15 minutes   *4–6 servings*

In 2-quart microwave-safe casserole combine:
>**½ cup butter**
>**1 tablespoon onion, minced**

Microwave uncovered on High for 2 minutes. Stir in:
>**2 tablespoons flour**

Add, blending well:
>**4 ounces mushrooms, sliced**
>**¼ cup dry vermouth or apple juice**
>**½ teaspoon salt**
>**⅛ teaspoon white pepper**
>**1 pound bay scallops**
>**1 bay leaf**
>**2 teaspoons lemon juice**

Stir carefully, cover, and microwave on High for 6 minutes or until scallops are tender. Remove bay leaf. Whisk together:
>**½ cup light cream**
>**1 egg yolk**

Gradually whisk some of the hot mixture into the egg and cream. When smooth, add that to the remaining sauce. Cover and microwave at 50% for 5 minutes.

Watch carefully and if the sauce begins to boil, stir immediately to avoid curdling or separation. If this condition does occur, more cream can be added to bring sauce back to normal consistency.

Seafood Newburg

Preparation Time: 15 minutes   *4–6 servings*

Substitute 1 pound of any seafood for the scallops in the Coquilles St. Jacques recipe above.

Serve on patty shells.

Seafood Casserole

Preparation Time: 15 minutes   *4 servings*

Combine in 1½-quart casserole, then cover with casserole lid and micro-wave on High for 3 minutes:

3 tablespoons green onions, sliced
½ cup celery, chopped

Stir in:

2 cans cream of mushroom soup
8 ounces small shrimp, peeled
6 ounces crab meat
½ cup cashews
2 cups chow mein noodles

Microwave on High for 3 minutes. Stir. Microwave on High for 2–3 minutes more.

Seafood Splash

Preparation Time: 17 minutes   *4–5 servings*

Partially thaw:

1 package (6 ounces) frozen crabmeat and shrimp

Combine in 1½-quart glass casserole:

2 cups shredded potatoes or 12 ounces frozen hash brown
potatoes, thawed
1 tablespoon butter or margarine
2 green onions, sliced (including tops)

Cover with casserole lid.

Microwave on High for 4½–5½ minutes, or until potatoes are almost tender, stirring once.

Stir in:

1 can (10¾ ounces) condensed cream of celery soup
¾ cup sour cream
1 tablespoon lemon juice
¼ teaspoon garlic salt

Add seafood. Cover.

Microwave on High for 4–5 minutes or until hot. Stir well.

Sprinkle with:

½ cup cheddar cheese, shredded
2 tablespoons sliced green olives, if desired
paprika

Microwave uncovered on High for 2–2½ minutes or until cheese is melted.

Fish Medley

Cut into matchstick pieces:
> **2 carrots**
> **2 potatoes**

Place in 1-quart casserole with:
> **2 tablespoons water**

Cover and microwave on High for 7–8 minutes. Season and set aside. Cut into serving-size pieces and arrange in 2-quart casserole over vegetables:
> **12 ounces fish**

Add:
> **3 tablespoons white wine or lemon juice**
> **½ lemon, sliced**
> **½ teaspoon salt**
> **dash pepper**

Microwave on High for 4 minutes or until fish flakes.

Fish Creole

Preparation Time: 25 minutes   *6 servings*

Combine in 2-quart casserole, then microwave on High for 4 minutes:
> **1 green pepper, sliced**
> **1½ cups green onions, sliced**
> **2 tablespoons butter**

Stir in:
> **2 cups tomatoes, cut up and drained**
> **1 cup tomato sauce**
> **½ teaspoon ground thyme**
> **1 bay leaf**
> **salt and pepper**

Arrange on top of sauce:
> **1½ pounds flounder fillets**

Cover with waxed paper. Microwave on High for 8 minutes. Let stand 5 minutes. Serve over cooked rice.

Bouillabaisse

Preparation Time: 30 minutes   *5–6 servings*

Combine in 2-quart glass casserole:

> **1 medium onion, chopped**
> **1 clove garlic, minced**
> **1 tablespoon vegetable oil**

Microwave uncovered on High for 3–4 minutes or until tender, stirring once.

Stir in:

> **1 can (28 ounces) whole tomatoes, undrained**
> **1 bay leaf**
> **1 teaspoon instant chicken bouillon**
> **½ teaspoon salt**
> **½ teaspoon thyme leaves**
> **⅛ teaspoon ground allspice, if desired**
> **6 drops tabasco sauce**

Microwave uncovered on High for 13–15 minutes or until flavors are blended, stirring once.

Cut into 1-inch pieces:

> **1 pound fish fillets (red snapper, turbot, or pike)**

To tomato mixture add fish and:

> **6 ounces frozen uncooked shrimp**

Cover.

Microwave on High for 7–7½ minutes or until fish flakes apart easily and shrimp are firm, stirring twice. Remove bay leaf. Garnish with parsley and lemon slices.

Note: Crab, lobster, or clams can be combined with fish. Frozen cooked shrimp can be substituted for uncooked shrimp. Timing will be very similar.

Fish and Broccoli Bake

Preparation Time: 30 minutes   *4–5 servings*

In microwave-safe container, microwave on High for 4–4½ minutes or until nearly tender:

1 package (10 ounces) frozen chopped broccoli

Drain and set aside.

Combine in 1½-quart glass casserole:

¼ cup butter or margarine

½ cup celery, chopped

2 tablespoons onion, chopped

Cover with casserole lid.

Microwave on High for 4–4½ minutes or until vegetables are almost tender. Stir in:

2 tablespoons flour

½ teaspoon salt

½ cup milk

3 tablespoons dry cooking sherry (optional; see below)

Microwave on High for 3–4 minutes or until mixture boils and thickens, stirring once or twice.

Stir in drained broccoli and:

½ cup (2 ounces) cheddar cheese, shredded

Cut into 1-inch pieces:

14–16 ounces fish fillets (turbot, snapper, or halibut)

Add broccoli mixture. Cover.

Microwave on High for 3½–4 minutes, stirring once.

Top with:

½ cup (2 ounces) cheddar cheese, shredded

Sprinkle with:

paprika

Microwave on High for 2–2½ minutes or until fish flakes apart easily with fork and mixture is bubbly.

Note: Frozen mixed vegetables can be substituted for broccoli. Sherry can be omitted; increase milk to ⅔ cup.

Hot Tuna Sandwiches

Preparation Time: 7 minutes   *6–8 servings*

Combine in small mixing bowl:
> **1 can (9½ ounces) tuna, drained**
> **½ cup celery, chopped**
> **¼ cup green onions, sliced**
> **1 cup (4 ounces) swiss or cheddar cheese, shredded**
> **3 hard-cooked eggs, chopped**
> **⅓ cup mayonnaise**
> **⅓ cup sour cream**
> **2 tablespoons chopped pimento, drained**
> **½ tablespoon lemon juice**

Mix well.

Cut in half lengthwise:
> **1 small loaf french bread (about 12 inches long)**

Scoop out center of bread leaving a 12-inch shell. Place crust-side down on glass serving plate. Fill each half with tuna mixture and garnish with parsley. Microwave uncovered on High for 2–2½ minutes or until heated, rotating plate once. Cut into 6–8 sections.

Note: The bread that is removed can be used for bread crumbs. Individual sandwiches can be made by using french rolls. To make less than six sandwiches, fill the number of rolls desired and refrigerate remaining filling. Microwave smaller quantity on High for 20–30 seconds for each sandwich.

Jiffy Tuna Casserole

Preparation Time: 20 minutes   *About 6 servings*

Combine in 1½-quart, microwave-safe casserole:

1 can (10¾ ounces) condensed mushroom soup
1 can (6½ ounces) water-packed light tuna, drained
1 can (2 ounces) sliced mushrooms, undrained
4 ounces uncooked egg noodles (about 2 cups)
1⅓ cups milk
1 cup frozen peas
⅛ teaspoon pepper

Cover with casserole lid. Microwave on High for 12–14 minutes or until noodles are tender and sauce is creamy, stirring twice. Let stand covered for 5 minutes.

Sprinkle with:

1 can (1¾ ounces) shoestring potatoes

Note: Peas can be omitted or other frozen vegetable substituted. Chow mein noodles or crushed potato chips (½ cup) can be substituted for shoestring potatoes. Cooked chicken (1½ cups, cubed) can be substituted for tuna.

QUICK BREADS AND YEAST BREADS

• All breads rise higher when baked in a microwave oven than in a conventional one.

• Reduce leavening ingredients by one-fourth to avoid a bitter aftertaste. however, do not change the amount of baking soda used if the recipe calls for sour cream or buttermilk.

• If leavening cannot be reduced, allow the batter to stand 10 minutes before baking so the gas can release.

• Because the breads rise so high, be sure to fill the pans only half-full to avoid the batter cooking over.

• Most quick breads cook best in a baking ring.

• Because of the short cooking time, little evaporation happens. Consequently, browning does not occur naturally. To create a browned appearance on your bread, follow one of these suggestions before baking:

> • brush top of dough with melted butter
> • top with brown sugar
> • top with crushed nuts or cereal
> • top with seeds or buttered onions
> • sprinkle with any color topping
> • top with crumbs made from mixing brown sugar, margarine, and flour
> • use a dark flour in the batter instead of white flour

• The most common mistake in making quick breads is overbaking. Follow power levels and baking times carefully.

• Breads are done when the dough recedes from the sides of the pan and springs back when gently touched (even though the surface may appear moist).

• Check for doneness also by inserting a wooden pick in the center of the dough, then checking to see if it comes out clean.

• After baking, cool breads for easier slicing.

• Reheat one piece or slice at a time, wrapped in a paper towel, on High for 15 seconds.

Muffin Mix

Prepare mix as directed on package.

Line muffin ring with paper baking cups. Fill half full with batter. Sprinkle tops with cinnamon sugar. Microwave on High for 2–3 minutes. Serve warm.

Muffins

Bran, Granola, Grapenuts, Oatmeal, or Wheat Germ

Preparation Time: 20 minutes   Yields 12 muffins

In 2-cup glass measure microwave on High for 1½ minutes:

> **⅓ cup water**

Stir in and let stand 10 minutes:

> **⅔ cup whole bran cereal, or granola, or grapenuts, or quick-cooking oatmeal, or toasted wheat germ**

Stir together in mixing bowl:

> **1¼ cups flour**
> **⅓ cup sugar**
> **2 teaspoons baking powder**
> **¼ teaspoon salt**
> **¼ teaspoon cinnamon**

Stir together, then stir into dry ingredients just until moistened:

> **1 beaten egg**
> **⅓ cup milk**
> **⅓ cup cooking oil**
> **softened cereal mixture**

Fold in:

> **1 small apple, cored and finely chopped or ⅓ cup dried, chopped apricots or raisins**
> **⅓ cup walnuts, or pecans chopped**

Fill paper-lined muffin cups half full with batter. Top with crumbs made by combining the following:

> **2 tablespoons nuts, chopped**
> **2 tablespoons flour**
> **1 tablespoon brown sugar**
> **1 tablespoon margarine, melted**

Microwave 6 at a time on High for 3 minutes or until a wooden pick inserted comes out clean.

Fruit and Spice Muffins

Preparation Time: 8 minutes   Yields 6 muffins

Combine in large mixing bowl:

        ⅔ cup flour
        3 tablespoons sugar
        1 teaspoon baking powder
        ¼ teaspoon salt
        ½ teaspoon cinnamon or pumpkin pie spice

Stir into dry ingredients just until moistened:

        1 egg yolk, beaten
        2 tablespoons oil
        2 tablespoons milk
        ⅓ cup applesauce, cooked pumpkin, or mashed bananas

Fold in:

        2 tablespoons nuts, chopped or sunflower seeds
        2 tablespoons raisins

Fill paper-lined muffin cups half full. Top with crumbs, chopped nuts, or seeds, or cinnamon sugar. Microwave 6 at a time on High for 3 minutes. Serve warm.

Low-Fat Cornbread

Preparation Time: 17 minutes   *6 servings*

Combine:
> **¾ cup skim milk**
> **1 teaspoon vinegar**

Mix well. Set aside.

Blend together in large mixing bowl:
> **⅓ cup cooking oil**
> **¼ cup sugar**

Beat in:
> **2 egg whites**

Stir in milk mixture.

Add:
> **1 cup unsifted all-purpose flour**
> **⅔ cup yellow cornmeal**
> **1 teaspoon baking powder**
> **½ teaspoon salt**
> **¼ teaspoon soda**

Mix until smooth.

Use a baking ring or grease bottom and sides of 8-inch round glass baking dish.

Sprinkle with:
> **cornflake crumbs**

If using a baking dish, place a custard cup open-end-up in center of baking dish. Spoon cornbread mixture around cup, spreading evenly.

Microwave uncovered on High for 6–7 minutes or until top is no longer doughy, rotating dish two or three times. Cool 5 minutes. Remove up and invert cornbread onto serving plate. Cut into wedges.

Note: If cornbread is cooked in baking ring, reduce microwave time to 5–6 minutes.

Fruity Nut Bread

Preparation Time: 30 minutes   Yields 2 loaves

Beat together in a large mixing bowl:

> **2 cups sugar**
> **1½ cups cooking oil**
> **3 eggs**
> **1 teaspoon vanilla**

Add:

> **2 cups strawberries, blueberries, or raspberries, thawed**
> **1 cup nuts, chopped**

Stir in:

> **3 cups flour**
> **1 teaspoon salt**
> **1 teaspoon baking soda**
> **1 teaspoon cinnamon**

Divide batter between two loaf pans which have been greased and coated with finely chopped nuts. Sprinkle chopped nuts on top. Cover with waxed paper and microwave one loaf at a time at 50% for 10 minutes, then on High for 2 minutes or until wooden pick inserted in center comes out clean.

Caramel Nut Sticky Buns

Preparation Time: 10 minutes   *6 servings*

Combine in 9-inch round baking pan:

3 tablespoons margarine

⅓ cup brown sugar

1 tablespoon water

1 teaspoon cinnamon

⅓ cup nuts, chopped

Microwave on High for 1 minute. Stir to combine, then add:

1 can refrigerator biscuits, each cut into quarters

Coat each piece in nut mixture. Place in pan, then microwave on High for 2–3 minutes.

Defrosting Frozen Dough

Fill 1-cup glass measure with water. Microwave on High for 3 minutes. Place frozen dough in greased loaf pan, then place in warm oven beside water. Microwave at 10% for 10 minutes. Turn dough over. Microwave at 10% for 10 more minutes. Allow to stand in oven for 30 minutes or until dough has risen 1 inch above pan and is ready to bake.

White Bread

Preparation Time: 60 minutes   *Yields 2 loaves*

Heavily butter 2 loaf pans.
Combine in large mixing bowl:

2½ cups all-purpose flour
2 packages dry yeast
2 tablespoons sugar
2 teaspoons salt

Combine in 4-cup glass measure and heat to 125°F using probe:

1 tablespoon margarine
2¼ cup milk

Stir liquid mixture into flour mixture and beat well. Knead in until smooth and satiny:

2¾ to 3½ cups flour

Place in greased bowl. To speed bread's rising, place dough in microwave beside 1 cup boiling water. Microwave at 10% for 10 minutes. Then allow to stand in oven for 20 minutes or until dough has doubled in size.

Form dough into desired shape. Place in greased pan and brush with melted butter to help achieve a more crisp, brown crust. Repeat above procedure so dough rises a second time.

Remove water and microwave bread on High for 6–7 minutes or until bread springs back. (Bread may also be baked in a conventional oven, especially if a harder, drier crust is desired.)

Whole Wheat Bread

Preparation Time: 60 minutes   *Yields 2 loaves*

Follow White Bread recipe (above), except use whole wheat flour in place of all-purpose flour and ¼ cup honey instead of sugar.

Rye Bread

Preparation Time: 60 minutes   Yields 2 loaves

Follow White Bread recipe (above), except use rye flour or pumpernickel flour in place of all-purpose flour and add to dry ingredients:

1 tablespoon caraway seeds

Oatmeal Bread

Preparation Time: 1 hour and 20 minutes   Yields 2 loaves

Combine and allow to stand:

½ cup warm water
2 packages active dry yeast

Combine in large glass mixing bowl and microwave on High for 3 minutes, uncovered:

1½ cups water
1 cup quick cooking oats

Stir in:

⅓ cup margarine
½ cup light molasses
1 tablespoon salt

Beat in:

2 eggs
2 cups flour

Stir in softened yeast and:

2 cups flour

Stir in an additional:

2 cups flour

Cover with plastic wrap. Microwave at 10% for 10 minutes. Let stand 20 minutes or until double in size. Stir down and divide into two buttered loaf pans. Follow same procedure to allow dough to rise again until double in size. Brush loaves with melted butter and sprinkle with wheat germ or cereal crumbs. Microwave one loaf at a time on High for 8–10 minutes, or until surface springs back when touched lightly.

Loaf English Muffins

Preparation Time: 30 minutes   Yields 2 loaves

Grease 2 glass loaf pans and coat with corn meal.
Combine in mixing bowl:

> **2 packages dry yeast**
> **3 cups flour**
> **1 tablespoon sugar**
> **2 teaspoons salt**
> **¼ teaspoon baking soda**

Combine in 4-cup glass measure and heat to 120°F using probe:

> **2 cups milk**
> **½ cup water**

Add liquid ingredients to dry. Beat well and stir in:

> **2 cups flour**

Divide batter between prepared loaf pans and sprinkle with corn meal.
Allow to rise. Cover with waxed paper and microwave each loaf separately
on High for 6–7 minutes. Loaf will look pale. Allow to stand 5 minutes.
Slice and toast.

Defrosting Frozen Breads, Muffins, and Coffee Cakes

An excellent way to keep breads fresh is to freeze them and only defrost
what is needed.

Because these baked products defrost very quickly, it is best to only partially defrost them rather than risk their being overcooked.

Wrap breads in paper towels to absorb excess moisture. Use the following
guidelines:

Food	Amount	Level	Time
Hamburger buns	1 pound	30%	3½ minutes
Hot dog buns	1 pound	30%	3½ minutes
Loaf of bread	1 pound	80%	1½ minutes
English muffins	2	High	30–45 seconds
Pancakes	2	High	30–45 seconds
Waffles	2	High	30–45 seconds
Coffee cake	12 ounces	80%	1½ minutes
Tortillas	2	High	15 seconds

CAKES, COOKIES, AND BARS

What You Ought to Know About Baking Cakes in a Microwave

- Cakes baked in a microwave oven will have a lighter texture and greater volume and be very moist.
- Since microwaved cakes do not brown, dust the greased baking dish with granulated sugar or finely ground nuts before pouring in batter.
- Since cakes rise higher when microwaved, pour in only enough batter to make the baking dish one-third to one-half full.
- For a special treat, divide the extra cake batter into cupcake pans or flat-bottomed ice cream cups and microwave on High for 50 seconds.
- Always cover a cake with waxed paper or a paper towel to allow steam to escape but to keep the heat in.
- Always start on the lower power level indicated so the cake doesn't get tough.
- Be careful not to overbake. Follow the shortest baking time suggested. Check with a tester, then bake the additional suggested time if needed.
- Frost or cover the cake as soon as possible after cooling, since a crustless cake tends to get stale quickly.
- Some items work better in conventional ovens. For example, chiffon and angel food cakes do not microwave well.
- Many cake mixes now include microwave directions.

Preparing a Basic Cake Mix

Because speed is important to most microwave-oven users, here are instructions for doing a basic cake mix, with a series of delicious variations.

"From scratch" cakes can also be done in a microwave oven although without the efficiency possible with a mix. So take your pick!

- Mix the ingredients together about 5 minutes before you plan to bake the cake so the leavening has a chance to react to the moisture before it is heated.
- Use 1 less egg than called for by the conventional instructions. The reason? The steam that is created in the microwave process produces extra leavening power.
- Use one-fourth less water than called for by the conventional instructions. In a conventional oven some of the moisture evaporates during the dry heat process, but in the shortened microwave process there is not time for this to happen.
- Fill the prepared pan only half full. With the extra volume

produced by the microwave process, this is essential or the batter will run over.

- Cover with waxed paper or a paper towel to keep the heat in the product while allowing the steam to escape.
- Depending on the mix the cake will bake in 10–15 minutes at 70%. After 10 minutes, test for doneness, then add more cooking time if necessary.
- To test for doneness, insert the tester into the center of the cake. If it comes out clean, the cake is done. The cake may appear moist and still be finished. The extra moisture will disappear during the standing time. If the cake begins to pull away from the sides of the pan, it is done.
- Usually a cake requires the same amount of standing time as baking time. If possible, let a cake stand in the oven because the extra heat on the bottom will help the extra moisture to evaporate.
- Frosting or glazing a cake is highly recommended, since a cake does not develop a crust and so has a tendency to become stale rather quickly.

Making Cupcakes

- Fill paper-lined muffin cups half full with cake batter.
- Microwave 6 cupcakes at a time, on High for 2–3 minutes, or until an inserted wooden pick comes out clean. (Flat-bottomed ice cream cups can be substituted for the cake papers.)

A Word about Baking Pans

Round pans bake better than square pans, because the food in the corners tends to dry out since it is hit first by the microwaves.

A tube pan is ideal. It distributes the heat more evenly due to the fact that microwaves cook from the outside in, as well as the inside out.

If you don't have a baking ring, a glass tumbler inverted in a large round casserole dish will serve the same purpose. On the other hand, baking rings are very inexpensive and can be used for more than just baking.

Preparing the Pan

Grease the pan as you would any baking pan. Sprinkle with an ingredient that will give the color and texture you desire for your finished product:

- Granulated sugar will produce a sweet crisp crust.
- Brownulated sugar will produce a sweet, brown, crisp crust.
- Cinnamon sugar will produce a spicy, sweet-flavored crust.
- Finely ground nuts, cereal, or graham cracker crumbs will produce a crisper, browner crust.

Defrosting a Frozen Cake

- Cakes defrost very quickly. But watch the time and power level to avoid producing a tough and rubbery texture.
- Defrost at 30% power.
- Cover with either waxed paper or a paper towel to retain moisture.
- A pound cake takes 2 minutes for a 10¾-ounce cake.
- A 2- or 3-layer cake weighing 1 pound takes 2–3 minutes.
- Cupcakes take 15 to 30 seconds apiece, if done one at a time.

Basic Cake Mix, adapted for a microwave oven

(Use these instructions for a cake mix in which the conventional directions call for 3 eggs, 1 cup water, ⅓ cup oil)
Preparation Time: 15 minutes   *Yields 1 cake*

Combine in mixing bowl:

2 eggs
¾ cup water
⅓ cup oil
1 cake mix

Pour into greased and sugar-sprinkled microwave-safe tube pan.
Microwave on High for 5 minutes. Microwave at 70% for 7 minutes more. Test for doneness.

Instant Glazed Cake

Preparation Time: 18 minutes   *Yields 1 cake*

Grease and sugar 12-cup microwave-safe baking ring.
In 2-cup glass measure microwave on High for 45 seconds:

¼ cup margarine

Add and mix well:

¾ cup preserves (orange or raspberry)
½ cup coconut, flaked

Spread evenly over the bottom of the prepared pan.
Spoon favorite prepared cake mix over top.
Cover and bake as directed for cake mix (above).

Dark Chocolate Cake

Preparation Time: 30 minutes   Yields 1 cake

In 8-cup glass measure microwave on High for 45 seconds:
>   **⅓ cup margarine**

Beat in:
>   **1 cup sugar**
>   **1 teaspoon vanilla**

Add and mix well:
>   **1 egg**
>   **1½ cups milk**
>   **1½ cups flour**
>   **½ cup unsweetened cocoa**
>   **½ teaspoon baking soda**
>   **½ teaspoon baking powder**
>   **½ teaspoon salt**

Pour evenly into greased and sugared pan and cover with waxed paper.
Microwave at 50% for 14 minutes. Test for doneness and microwave in 1
minute increments until tester comes out clean (surface will look moist.).
Let stand 10 minutes. Frost or cover as soon as cool.

Easy Chocolate Frosting

Preparation Time: 6 minutes   Yields 1¾ cup

Combine in 4-cup glass measuring cup and microwave on High for
3–4 minutes, stirring twice during that time:
>   **1 cup sugar**
>   **¼ cup margarine**
>   **¼ cup milk**

Then stir in:
>   **⅔ cup chocolate pieces**

Stir 2 or 3 times until thickened, then spread on cake.

Vanilla Frosting

Preparation Time: 5 minutes   Yields frosting for one layer cake

Soften (without melting) in microwave at 30% for 1 minute:
>   **3 tablespoons butter**

Beat in:
>   **1 cup confectioner's sugar, sifted**
>   **1 tablespoon light cream**

When smooth, stir in:
>   **¾ teaspoon vanilla**

Spread over cake before frosting hardens.

Peanut Butter Frosting

Preparation Time: 5 minutes   Yields frosting for one layer cake

In 4-cup glass microwave-safe measuring bowl microwave at 50% for 1–2 minutes, or until mixture comes to boil:
>   **2 tablespoons butter or margarine**
>   **2 tablespoons peanut butter**
>   **2 tablespoons milk or cream**
>   **⅛ teaspoon salt**

Stir in:
>   **2 cups confectioner's sugar**
>   **½ teaspoon vanilla**

Beat until smooth. Spread over cake before frosting hardens.

Pound Cake

Preparation Time: 20 minutes   Yields 1 cake

Grease glass loaf pan, then sprinkle with finely ground almonds.
Microwave in glass mixing bowl for 30 seconds:

½ cup butter

Cream in:

1 cup sugar
2 eggs

Add and mix until smooth:

½ cup milk
½ teaspoon vanilla
1¼ cups flour
½ teaspoon baking powder
¼ teaspoon salt

Spoon batter evenly into prepared loaf pan. Cover with waxed paper. Microwave at 50% for 10 minutes. Test for doneness and microwave on High for 30 second increments until tester inserted in center comes out clean.

Crowned Pound Cake

Preparation Time: 35 minutes   Yields   1 cake

Microwave on High for 15–20 seconds:

⅓ cup butter

Stir in:

2 tablespoons brown sugar
½ cup pecans, chopped
¾ cup vanilla wafers, crushed

Grease bottom and sides of glass loaf dish, then line the bottom with waxed paper. Pat topping evenly into bottom and up the sides. In glass measuring bowl, microwave on High for 20 to 30 seconds:

½ cup butter

Cream in:

1 cup sugar
2 eggs

Add and mix until smooth:

½ cup milk
½ teaspoon vanilla
1¼ cups flour
½ teaspoon baking powder

Cakes, Cookies, and Bars

¼ teaspoon salt

Pour batter evenly into prepared pan. Microwave at 50% power for 10 minutes, then on High for 2–3 minutes or until an inserted toothpick comes out clean. Cool 15 minutes. Serve with ice cream.

Poppy Seed Ring Cake

Preparation Time: 25 minutes   *10–12 servings*

Combine in a large mixing bowl:

1 package (18½ ounces) yellow cake mix
1 package (3¾ ounces) lemon instant pudding and pie filling mix
4 eggs
½ cup cooking oil
1 cup water (less 1½ tablespoons)
⅓ cup poppy seeds

Beat mixture at low speed with an electric mixer until ingredients are moistened, then beat on high speed 3–4 minutes. If beating by hand, stir until ingredients are moistened; then beat about 150 strokes per minute for 3–4 minutes. Butter the bottom and sides of a 10-cup glass or plastic ring mold with:

1 tablespoon butter or margarine

Mix and sprinkle on bottom and sides:

1 tablespoon cinnamon
3 tablespoons granulated sugar

Remove 1 cup of batter from bowl and save to make cupcakes. Pour remaining batter into mold.

Microwave at 50% for 10 minutes then on High for 2 minutes. Let cake stand in oven 5 minutes until it begins to pull away from sides. Remove from oven and invert cake onto serving plate.

Creme de Menthe Cake

Preparation Time: 20 minutes   *Yields 1 cake*

Grease and sugar 12-cup baking ring.
Combine in large mixer bowl:

> **1 package (18½ ounces) yellow cake mix**
> **1 package (3½ ounces) pistachio pudding mix**
> **1 cup cooking oil**
> **¾ cup water**
> **¼ cup creme de menthe**
> **4 eggs**

Blend until moistened, then beat 3 minutes. Pour evenly into prepared pan.
Pour over batter and stir to marble:

> **½ cup chocolate syrup**

Cover with waxed paper. Microwave at 50% for 12 minutes, then on High for 3–4 minutes or until a wooden pick comes out clean. Let stand in microwave for 10 minutes. Cool. Frost.

Piña Colada Cake

Combine in large mixer bowl:

> **1 package (18½ ounces) yellow cake mix**
> **1 package (3½ ounces) coconut pudding mix**
> **1 cup cooking oil**
> **¾ cup water**
> **¼ cup dark rum or 1 tablespoon rum flavoring**
> **4 eggs**

Blend until moistened, then beat 3 minutes. Pour evenly into prepared 9 × 13 pan. Cover with waxed paper. Microwave at 50% for 12 minutes, then on High for 3–4 minutes or until a wooden pick comes out clean. Let stand 10 minutes. Frost with frosting made by combining:

> **1 package coconut pudding mix**
> **1 container whipped topping**
> **1 can crushed pineapple**
> **¼ cup dark rum or 1 tablespoon rum flavoring**

Thumbprint Cookies

Preparation Time: 10 minutes   Yields   36–40 cookies

Beat together to form firm dough:
> **½ cup butter, softened**
> **¼ cup brown sugar**
> **1 egg**
> **1 teaspoon vanilla**
> **1½ cups flour**
> **¼ teaspoon salt**
> **1½ cups coconut**

Form into ¾ inch balls, then place 16 cookies in a circle on microwave baking sheet or piece of cardboard. Flatten each cookie with thumb. Microwave on High for 2–4 minutes. Fill imprints with jelly or icing.

Hello Dolly's

Preparation Time: 25 minutes   Yields 24 bars

In 9-inch round dish microwave on High for 1½ minutes:
> **6 tablespoons butter**

Spread over melted butter:
> **1 cup graham cracker crumbs**

Sprinkle over crumbs:
> **3½ ounces coconut, grated**

Layer:
> **6 ounces chocolate chips**
> **6 ounces peanut butter chips**
> **1 cup nuts, chopped**

Pour over all:
> **1 can sweetened condensed milk (see page 181)**

Microwave at 70% for 9–10 minutes. Let stand 10 minutes.

Peanut Butter Bars

Preparation Time: 20 minutes   Yields   24 bars

Blend until smooth:
> **1 cup margarine, softened**
> **1 cup brown sugar**
> **¼ cup peanut butter**

Mix in until combined:
> **1¾ cups flour**
> **1 cup rolled oats**
> **½ teaspoon baking soda**

Press mixture into greased 8 × 12 inch glass baking pan. Microwave at 70% for 7–9 minutes or until puffed in center. Set aside. Combine in glass measure and microwave on High for 2–3 minutes or until melted:
> **⅓ cup semi-sweet chocolate pieces**
> **3 tablespoons peanut butter**

Spread over baked bars. Cool and cut.

Coconut Macaroons

Preparation Time: 12 minutes   Yields 3 dozen cookies

Combine in 2-quart glass mixing bowl:
> **2⅔ cups flaked coconut**
> **⅔ cup sweetened condensed milk (see recipe on page 181 or use half a can prepared milk)**
> **1 teaspoon vanilla or almond extract**

Microwave on High for 2 minutes. Stir. Microwave on High another 2 minutes. Stir. Microwave on High 2 minutes more or until mixture loses its gloss. Immediately spoon onto wax paper and shape into balls. Store in airtight container.

Chewy Gooey Bars

Preparation Time: 15 minutes   *Yields 24 bars*

Combine in 2-quart glass measure:
> **2 cups quick-cooking rolled oats**
> **½ cup margarine**

Microwave on High for 3–4 minutes and stir in:
> **½ cup brown sugar, packed**
> **¼ cup light corn syrup**

Microwave on High for 2–3 minutes or until sugar is melted, then press mixture into buttered baking dish.

Place in 1-cup glass measure and microwave on High for 2 minutes or until smooth when stirred:
> **⅓ cup semi-sweet chocolate pieces**
> **2 tablespoons peanut butter**

Spread over warm mixture. Chill and cut into squares.

Favorite Chocolate Brownies

Preparation Time: 20 minutes   *8–10 servings*

Place in 1-quart glass mixing bowl:
> **¼ cup butter or margarine**

Microwave uncovered on High for 15–20 seconds or until softened.
Blend in:
> **½ cup sugar**

Add, one at a time, beating after each:
> **2 eggs**

Blend in:
> **½ teaspoon vanilla**

Add:
> **½ cup unsifted all-purpose flour**
> **½ cup chocolate-flavored ice cream syrup**
> **¼ teaspoon salt**

Mix well. If desired, add ⅓ cup chopped nuts.

Grease bottom only of 8-inch square microwave-safe baking dish. Spread batter in dish and cover loosely with plastic wrap.

Microwave on High for 5–6 minutes or until no longer doughy, rotating dish once or twice. Let stand in microwave oven for 10 minutes. Uncover and cool. Cut into squares.

Cherry-Chocolate Brownies

Preparation Time: 20 minutes   *8–10 servings*

Place in 1-quart glass mixing bowl:
> **⅓ cup butter or margarine**

Microwave uncovered on High for 45–60 seconds or until melted.
Stir in:
> **⅓ cup unsweetened cocoa**
> **1 cup sugar**

Add, one at a time, beating after each:
> **2 eggs**

Blend in:
> **½ teaspoon vanilla**

Add:
> **¾ cup unsifted all-purpose flour**
> **½ teaspoon baking powder**

Mix well. Grease bottom only of 8-inch square microwave-safe baking
dish. Spread batter in dish.
Sprinkle with:
> **⅓ cup maraschino cherries, chopped**

Cover loosely with plastic wrap. Microwave on High for 5–6 minutes or
until no longer doughy, rotating dish once or twice. Let stand in microwave oven for 10 minutes. Uncover, cool, and cut into squares.

Chewy Butterscotch Brownies

Preparation Time: 20 minutes | *8–10 servings*

Place in 1-quart glass mixing bowl:

⅓ cup butter or margarine

Microwave uncovered on High for 20–30 seconds or until softened.
Blend in:

1 cup packed brown sugar

Add, one at a time, beating after each:

2 eggs

Blend in:

1 teaspoon vanilla

Add:

1 cup unsifted all-purpose flour
½ teaspoon baking powder
¼ teaspoon salt

Mix well.
Stir in:

½ cup nuts, chopped
¼ cup butterscotch pieces

Grease bottom only of 8-inch square microwave-safe baking dish. Spread batter in dish.
Sprinkle with:

¼ cup butterscotch pieces (additional)

Cover loosely with plastic wrap.
Microwave on High for 5–6 minutes or until no longer doughy, rotating dish once or twice. Let stand in microwave oven for 10 minutes. Uncover and cool. Cut into squares.

Peanut Butter Brownies

Preparation Time: 25 minutes   *8–10 servings*

Combine in 1-quart glass mixing bowl:
> **2 squares (2 ounces) unsweetened chocolate**
> **¼ cup butter or margarine**

Microwave uncovered on High for 1–1½ minutes or until melted, stirring once.
Blend in:
> **1 cup sugar**

Add, one at a time, beating after each:
> **2 eggs**

Blend in:
> **½ teaspoon vanilla**

Add:
> **¾ cup unsifted all-purpose flour**
> **½ teaspoon baking powder**
> **¼ teaspoon salt**

Mix well. Grease bottom only of 8-inch square microwave-safe baking dish. Spread batter in dish. Set aside.
Place in 1-cup glass measure:
> **⅓ cup chunky or creamy peanut butter**

Microwave uncovered on High for 1–1½ minutes or until hot, stirring once. Spoon over batter. Cover loosely with plastic wrap.
Microwave on High for 5–6 minutes or until no longer doughy, rotating dish once or twice. Let stand in microwave oven for 10 minutes. Uncover, cool, and cut into squares. If desired, frost and top with crushed peanuts.

Macadamia Nut Brownies

Preparation Time: 20 minutes   *8–10 servings*

Combine in 1-quart glass mixing bowl:
> **6 tablespoons butter or margarine**
> **½ cup semi-sweet chocolate pieces**

Microwave uncovered on High for 1–1½ minutes or until melted, stirring once.
Blend in:
> **1 cup sugar**

Add, one at a time, beating after each:
> **2 eggs**

Blend in:
> **1 teaspoon vanilla**

Add:
> **1½ cups unsifted all-purpose flour**
> **½ teaspoon baking powder**
> **¼ teaspoon salt**

Mix well.
Stir in:
> **⅓ cup macadamia nuts, coarsely chopped**

Grease bottom only of 8-inch square microwave-safe baking dish. Spread batter in dish. Cover loosely with plastic wrap.
Microwave on High for 5–6 minutes or until no longer doughy, rotating dish once or twice. Let stand in microwave oven for 10 minutes. Uncover and cool.
Sprinkle with:
> **powdered sugar**

Cut into squares.

Note: Other nuts can be substituted for macadamia nuts.

Rocky Ridge Brownies

Preparation Time: 25 minutes   *8–10 servings*

Combine in 1-quart glass mixing bowl:

1½ squares (1½ ounces) unsweetened chocolate
⅓ cup butter or margarine

Microwave uncovered on High for 1–1½ minutes or until melted, stirring once.

Blend in:

1 cup sugar

Add, one at a time, beating after each:

2 eggs

Blend in:

1 teaspoon vanilla

Add:

1 cup unsifted all-purpose flour
½ teaspoon baking powder
¼ teaspoon salt

Mix well.

Stir in:

¼ cup pecans or walnuts, chopped

Grease bottom only of 8-inch square microwave-safe baking dish. Spread batter in dish. Cover loosely with plastic wrap.

Microwave on High for 5–6 minutes or until no longer doughy, rotating dish once or twice.

Sprinkle evenly with:

2 cups miniature marshmallows

Cover and let stand in microwave oven for 10 minutes. Uncover and cool. Meanwhile, combine in 2-cup glass measure:

½ square (½ ounce) unsweetened chocolate
1 tablespoon butter or margarine

Microwave uncovered on High for 45–60 seconds or until melted, stirring once.

Beat in:

½ cup unsifted powdered sugar
¼ teaspoon vanilla

Add, until of a glaze consistency:

1–2 teaspoons hot water

Drizzle evenly over brownies. Cool completely. Cut into squares using knife dipped in hot water.

Macaroon Brownies

Preparation Time: 20 minutes	8–10 servings

Combine in 1-quart glass bowl:

> **2 squares (2 ounces) unsweetened chocolate**
> **¼ cup butter or margarine**

Microwave uncovered on High for 1–1½ minutes or until melted, stirring once. Blend in:

> **1 cup sugar**

Add, one at a time, beating after each:

> **2 eggs**

Blend in:

> **1 teaspoon vanilla**

Add:

> **¾ cup unsifted all-purpose flour**
> **½ teaspoon baking powder**

Mix well. Grease 10 × 6-inch microwave-safe baking dish on bottom only. Spread batter in dish. Set aside.
Combine:

> **1 cup coconut, flaked**
> **¼ cup light corn syrup**
> **1 tablespoon flour**
> **1 tablespoon half and half or milk**
> **¼ teaspoon almond extract**

Mix well. Drop by teaspoonsful onto bars. Swirl knife through batter several times. Cover loosely with plastic wrap.
Microwave on High for 5½–6½ minutes or until no longer doughy, rotating dish once or twice. Let stand in microwave oven for 10 minutes.
Uncover and cool. If desired, frost with favorite chocolate frosting. Cut into squares and serve.

Note: If desired, add ⅓ cup chopped nuts to batter just before spreading in pan.

Cream Cheese Brownies

Preparation Time: 25 minutes   *8–10 servings*

Place in 1-quart glass mixing bowl:
>   **½ cup butter or margarine**

Microwave uncovered on High for 20–30 seconds or until softened.
Blend in:
>   **1 cup sugar**

Add, one at a time, beating after each:
>   **2 eggs**

Blend in:
>   **1 teaspoon vanilla**

Add:
>   **¾ cup unsifted all-purpose flour**
>   **⅓ cup unsweetened cocoa**
>   **½ teaspoon baking powder**
>   **¼ teaspoon salt**

Mix well. Grease bottom only of 8-inch square microwave-safe baking dish. Spread half of batter in dish. Set aside.
Place in 2-cup glass measure:
>   **1 package (3 ounces) cream cheese**

Microwave on High for 30–45 seconds or until softened.
Blend in:
>   **1 tablespoon sugar**

Spoon over batter in dish. Spoon remaining batter evenly over top. Cut through batter with knife several times to marble. Cover loosely with plastic wrap. Microwave on High for 5½–6½ minutes or until no longer doughy, rotating dish once or twice. Let stand in microwave oven for 10 minutes. Uncover and cool. Cut into squares.

Caramel Brownies

Preparation Time: 23 minutes   *8–10 servings*

Combine in 1-quart glass mixing bowl:
> **2 squares (2 ounces) unsweetened chocolate**
> **½ cup butter or margarine**

Microwave uncovered on High for 1–1½ minutes or until melted, stirring once.

Blend in:
> **½ cup sugar**
> **½ cup packed brown sugar**

Add, one at a time, beating after each:
> **2 eggs**

Blend in:
> **1 teaspoon vanilla**

Add:
> **1 cup unsifted all-purpose flour**
> **½ teaspoon baking powder**

Mix well. Grease bottom only of 8-inch square microwave-safe baking dish. Spread half of batter in dish.

Drizzle with:
> **½ cup caramel ice cream topping**

Sprinkle with:
> **⅓ cup nuts, chopped**

Spoon remaining batter evenly over caramel and nuts. Cover loosely with plastic wrap.

Microwave on High for 5½–6½ minutes or until no longer doughy, rotating dish once or twice. Let stand in microwave oven for 10 minutes. Uncover and cool. Cut into squares.

PIES AND DESSERTS

Apple or Peach Crumb Pie

Preparation Time: 20 minutes   *6–8 servings*

Cover bottom of unbaked 9-inch pie crust with dried beans or rice or set an empty glass casserole dish within it. Then microwave crust on High for 3–5 minutes.
Peel and slice:

2 pounds apples or peaches

Sprinkle fruit with:

2 teaspoons lemon juice

Combine and toss with fruit:

½ cup brown sugar
½ tablespoon cornstarch
½ teaspoon cinnamon

Arrange in pie crust. Cover with waxed paper and microwave on High for 4–6 minutes or until fruit is tender. Sprinkle with crumb topping made by combining:

½ cup flour
⅓ cup brown sugar
¼ cup margarine, softened
¼ teaspoon cinnamon
⅓ cup nuts, finely chopped (optional)

Microwave on High for 4–6 minutes or until set.

Pecan Pie

Preparation Time: 35 minutes   Yields   1 pie

In a medium glass mixing bowl, microwave at 70% for 1 minute, or until melted:

3 tablespoons butter or margarine

Stir in and mix well:

3 eggs, slightly beaten
1 cup dark corn syrup
¼ cup brown sugar
1½ teaspoons all-purpose flour
1 teaspoon vanilla
1½ cups pecan halves

Pour filling into 9-inch unbaked shell. Microwave at 30% for 25 to 30 minutes or until knife inserted near the center comes out clean. Cool.

Lemon Meringue Pie

Preparation Time: 15 minutes   *6–8 servings*

Combine:

2¼ cups sugar
½ cup cornstarch

Stir in:

2¼ cups water

Microwave on High for 3 minutes. Stir.
Beat and gradually combine with hot mixture:

4 egg yolks

Microwave on High for 2 minutes. Stir. Microwave on High 2 more
minutes. Stir. Continue process until mixture thickens.
Stir in:

¼ cup butter
⅜ cup lemon juice
⅛ cup lemon rind

Pour into:

9″ baked pie crust

Top with meringue made by beating to soft peaks:

3 egg whites
¼ teaspoon cream of tartar

Add and beat until stiff peaks form:

¾ teaspoon vanilla
6 tablespoons sugar

Microwave on High for 2 minutes until egg whites are set. The meringue
will not brown unless it is sprayed with a solution made by dissolving
brown sugar in water.
Note: Microwave lemon for 20 seconds before squeezing to release more
juice. Also, scrape the outside of the lemon before squeezing with a sharp
paring knife to release the oils which contain the flavor of the rind. Use
these oils rather than the rind for a smoother filling.

Lemon Chiffon Pie

Preparation Time: 7 minutes   *6–8 servings*

Beat until stiff and set aside:

4 egg whites
½ cup sugar

Combine until softened:

1 tablespoon unflavored gelatin

> **½ cup cold water**

In 2-quart glass measure combine:

> **4 egg yolks**
> **½ cup sugar**
> **½ cup lemon juice**
> **½ teaspoon salt**

Microwave on High for 2 minutes. Stir in softened gelatin mixture and:

> **1 tablespoon lemon rind**

Fold in egg-white mixture and serve in:

> **9-inch baked pie shell**

Coconut Cream Pie

Preparation Time: 30 minutes   *Yields   1 pie*

Combine in a 9-inch glass pie pan:

> **1 square semi-sweet chocolate**
> **¼ cup butter**

Microwave on High for 1–1½ minutes. Stir in:

> **2 cups coconut, flaked**

Microwave on High for 2–2½ minutes. Cool. Press into crust, reserving ½ cup.

Combine in 1-quart glass measure:

> **½ cup sugar**
> **¼ cup cornstarch**
> **2 cups milk**
> **½ teaspoon salt**

Microwave on High for 7–8 minutes, or until mixture thickens and boils. Stir twice.

Beat:

> **2 eggs**

Gradually stir warm mixture into eggs.

Microwave on High for 1 minute until mixture bubbles. Stir in:

> **2 tablespoons butter**
> **2 tablespoons rum or ½ teaspoon rum flavoring**

Cool 15 minutes. Spoon into coconut crust and top with whipped topping and reserved coconut mixture.

Coconut Custard Pie

Preparation Time: 20 minutes   8–10 minutes

Beat until smooth in mixer or blender:

> **¼ cup butter**
> **4 eggs**
> **2 cups milk**
> **¼ cup honey**
> **½ cup flour**
> **½ teaspoon baking powder**
> **½ teaspoon salt**
> **1½ teaspoons vanilla**
> **1½ teaspoons orange peel, grated**
> **¼ cup orange juice**

Stir in:

> **1 cup coconut, flaked**

Pour into greased 9- or 10-inch glass pie plate. Top with cinnamon sugar. Microwave on High for 8–10 minutes or until edges are set, then at 50% for 5–6 minutes or until center is puffed and set.

Pumpkin Pie Bake

Preparation Time: 20 minutes   6–8 servings

Combine in blender and blend for 1 minute:

> **¾ cup evaporated milk**
> **¾ cup sugar**
> **½ cup buttermilk baking mix**
> **2 tablespoons butter**
> **2 eggs**
> **2 cups processed pumpkin**
> **2½ teaspoons pumpkin pie spice**
> **2 teaspoons vanilla**

Pour into greased 9-inch glass pie plate. Cover with tented waxed paper. Microwave on High for 8 to 10 minutes or until edges are set, then at 50% for 5–6 minutes or until center is set.

Grasshopper Pie

Preparation Time: 40 minutes   *6–8 servings*

To form crust, microwave in a 9-inch glass pie plate on High for 30 seconds:

3 tablespoons butter or margarine

Stir in:

1½ cups (15–20) chocolate cream-filled cookies, crumbled

Press into bottom and up the sides of dish. Microwave on High for 2 minutes. Cool. Set aside.

In a large mixing bowl combine:

30 large or 3 cups miniature marshmallows

½ cup milk

Microwave on High for 2 minutes or until marshmallows begin to puff. Stir. If marshmallows are not completely melted, cook a few more seconds.

Stir in:

2–3 tablespoons creme de cocoa

2–3 tablespoons green creme de menthe

Cool about 30 minutes, until mixture is thickened but not set. Fold in:

1 cup whipping cream, whipped

Pour mixture into cooled crust. Refrigerate 4–6 hours or until well chilled. Garnish with whipped cream and chocolate curls if desired.

Note: You may use white creme de menthe, but, if you do, add 4–5 drops green food coloring. This pie will not keep for more than 2 days.

Fruit Crisp

Preparation Time: 15 minutes   *6–8 servings*

Microwave on High for 30 seconds in 2-quart glass measure:

¼ cup margarine

Stir in until crumbly:

¾ cup brown sugar

¾ cup flour

2 tablespoons coconut, flaked

2 tablespoons nuts, chopped

1 teaspoon cinnamon

Combine ½ of crumb mixture with:

4 cups apples, cherries, or peaches

Place in round baking dish. Top with remaining crumbs. Cover with waxed paper. Microwave on High for 10–12 minutes or until set.

Apple Crisp

Preparation Time: 20 minutes   *6–8 servings*

Combine in 8-inch square pan:
> **5 cups apples, sliced**
> **½ cup raisins**

Cover with plastic wrap and microwave on High for 5–6 minutes. Set aside.

In small mixing bowl combine:
> **1 cup flour**
> **½ cup sugar**
> **½ teaspoon baking powder**
> **¼ teaspoon salt**
> **1 egg**

Mix until crumbly and sprinkle over apples. Set aside.

Microwave in 1-cup glass measure for 30 seconds:
> **⅓ cup butter**

Drizzle over crumbs then sprinkle with:
> **cinnamon**

Microwave on High for 5–6 minutes or until topping is no longer doughy.

Fast and Fluffy Orange Pie

Preparation Time: 25 minutes   *8 servings*

Combine in 2-quart glass bowl:
> **4½ cups miniature marshmallows**
> **¾ cup orange juice**

Microwave uncovered on High for 2½–3½ minutes or until marshmallows are melted, stirring twice.

If desired, stir in:
> **1 tablespoon grated orange peel**

Place in freezer 15–20 minutes or until slightly thickened, stirring once or twice.

Fold in:
> **1 carton (8 ounces) thawed frozen whipped topping (about 3½ cups)**

Spoon into:
> **9-inch prepared graham cracker crust**

Refrigerate.

Quick Cherry Crunch

Preparation Time: 17 minutes   6–8 servings

Spread evenly in 8-inch square baking dish:
> **1 can cherry pie filling**

Combine in bowl and sprinkle over pie filling:
> **1 package single-layer yellow cake mix**
> **¼ cup nuts, chopped**
> **2 tablespoons brown sugar**
> **2 teaspoons cinnamon**

Melt and pour over top:
> **½ cup butter, melted**

Cover with waxed paper and microwave on High for 12–14 minutes or until topping is no longer doughy.

Custards and Puddings
A Simple Process, An Excellent Result

- Stirring is needed only once or twice to eliminate lumps.
- There is no need to place custards in steaming water.
- Quick puddings may be cooked on High.
- Pies or large custards should be microwaved at 50–70%.
- Cook a custard for the shortest amount of suggested time. Then allow it to stand until set (it will appear very loose but should set during standing time). When the standing time is up, insert a knife into the center of the custard. If it comes out clean, it is done; if it does not, microwave the additional time suggested in the recipe.
- Sprinkle tops of finished puddings and custards with your favorite spice to create an appealing color.

A General Time Guideline

Food	Amount	Power	Time
Pudding Mix	3¼ ounces	High	6–7 minutes
Egg Custard	3 ounces	70%	8–10 minutes
Tapioca	3¼ ounces	High	6–7 minutes

Vanilla Pudding

Preparation Time: 5 minutes   *2 servings*

Combine in 2-cup measure:
>**1 cup milk**
>**1 egg**
>**1 tablespoon cornstarch**
>**2 tablespoons sugar**

Microwave on High for 45 seconds. Stir. Microwave on High another 45 seconds. Stir. Microwave on High again for 45 seconds. Stir in:
>**¼ teaspoon vanilla**
>**small pat butter**

Chill and serve with fruit.

Chocolate Pudding

Preparation Time: 5 minutes   *2 servings*

Combine in 2-cup measure:
>**1 cup milk**
>**1 square semi-sweet chocolate**
>**1 tablespoon and 1 teaspoon cornstarch**
>**2 tablespoons sugar**

Microwave on High for 45 seconds. Stir. Microwave on High another 45 seconds. Stir. Microwave on High again for 45 seconds. Stir in:
>**¼ teaspoon vanilla**
>**small pat butter**

Chill and serve with whipped topping.

Rice Pudding

Preparation Time: 45 minutes   *8–10 servings*

Combine in 2-quart casserole:

    4 cups milk
    1 cup regular rice, uncooked
    ½ cup sugar
    ½ teaspoon salt (optional)

Cover and microwave on High for 9–10 minutes. Microwave at 30% for 30–35 minutes or until liquid is absorbed.

Stir in:

    2 tablespoons butter

Top with:

    cinnamon or nutmeg

Instant Rice Pudding

Preparation Time: 11 minutes   *8–10 servings*

Combine in 2-quart glass measure:

    3 cups milk
    1¾ cups instant rice
    ⅔ cup sugar
    2 tablespoons cornstarch

Microwave on High for 3 minutes. Stir. Microwave on High 3 more minutes. Stir. Microwave on High an additional 3 minutes.

Stir in:

    2 tablespoons butter
    1 teaspoon vanilla

Piña Colada Rice Pudding

Preparation Time: 25 minutes   *8 servings*

Combine in 2-quart glass measure:
> **2 cups rice, cooked**
> **2 cups milk**
> **¼ cup cream of coconut or sugar**
> **¼ teaspoon salt**

Microwave on High for 15 minutes, stirring once. Add:
> **2 tablespoons rum or 1½ teaspoons rum flavoring**

Set pudding aside.
Combine in 1-quart glass measure:
> **1 teaspoon cornstarch**
> **2 tablespoons brown sugar**
> **1 8-ounce can pineapple chunks with juice**

Microwave on High for 2 minutes. Stir. Microwave on High another 2 minutes. Stir in:
> **1 teaspoon butter**
> **2 tablespoons rum or 1½ teaspoons rum flavoring**

Spoon pudding into serving dishes. Top with pineapple sauce and **¼ cup toasted coconut.**

Tapioca Pudding

Preparation Time: 12 minutes   *8 servings*

Combine in 2-quart measure:
> **2 cups milk**
> **⅓ cup sugar**
> **¼ cup quick-cooking tapioca**
> **¼ teaspoon salt**
> **2 egg yolks, beaten**

Microwave on High for 5–6 minutes, stirring twice during that time.
Beat until frothy:
> **2 egg whites**

Gradually beat in until stiff peaks form:
> **2 tablespoons sugar**

Fold egg whites into cooked pudding just until combined.

Note: For an interesting twist fold in 2 tablespoons lemon or orange juice with egg whites.

Berry Fast Tapioca

Preparation Time: 7 minutes   *6 servings*

Combine in 2-quart glass bowl:

1 package (3½ ounces) tapioca pudding mix
1 cup water

Mix well. Microwave uncovered on High for 3–3½ minutes or until mixture boils and thickens, stirring once. Set aside.

Microwave on High for 45–60 seconds or until partially thawed:

1 package (10 ounces) frozen sweetened raspberries or strawberries

Add to hot pudding. Stir occasionally until thawed.

Fold in:

1 carton (4 ounces) thawed frozen whipped topping (about 1¾ cups)

Refrigerate.

Floating Island

Preparation Time: 15 minutes   *6 servings*

Combine in 4-cup glass measure:

⅔ cup sugar
1 tablespoon cornstarch
¼ teaspoon salt
2 cups milk

Microwave on High for 4–6 minutes or until boiling. Gradually stir into:

3 eggs yolks, beaten

Microwave on High for 2 minutes, stirring every 30 seconds.
Pour into shallow 1-quart casserole and chill 15 minutes.
In clean bowl beat until frothy:

3 egg whites
¼ teaspoon cream of tartar or salt

Gradually add:

⅓ cup sugar
½ teaspoon vanilla

Beat until stiff peaks form. Spoon onto cooled custard. Microwave on High for 2 minutes until egg whites are set. Serve warm or cold.

Vanilla Custard

Preparation Time: 12 minutes   6 servings

Combine in 2-quart glass measure:
> **⅔ cup sugar**
> **2½ tablespoons cornstarch**
> **1 tablespoon flour**
> **½ teaspoon salt**

Slowly stir in:
> **3 cups milk**

Microwave on High for 3 minutes. Stir. Microwave on High another 3 minutes. Stir. Microwave on High again for 3 minutes. Slowly blend some of the hot mixture into:
> **3 egg yolks, beaten**

When the temperature of the egg mixture reaches that of the hot milk mixture, combine the two mixtures gradually. Microwave on High for 1 minute and stir in:
> **1 tablespoon butter**
> **1 teaspoon vanilla**

Cover the surface with plastic wrap to prevent skin from forming.

Chocolate Custard

Preparation Time: 12 minutes   6 servings

Make Vanilla Custard recipe. During final step, stir in 1–1½ squares melted unsweetened chocolate squares with butter and vanilla.

Pumpkin Custard

Preparation Time: 25 minutes   *6–8 servings*

Microwave in 2-cup glass measure for 2½ minutes
> **1¾ cups milk**

Blend in:
> **4 eggs, beaten**
> **1 cup pumpkin, cooked**
> **⅓ cup sugar**
> **1 teaspoon vanilla**
> **¼ teaspoon salt**

Sprinkle with:
> **nutmeg**

Microwave at 50% for 18–20 minutes. Garnish with:
> **whipped cream**

Chocolate Mousse

Preparation Time: 6 minutes   *6 servings*

Measure into blender jar:
> **¼ cup cold water**
> **1 envelope gelatin**

Set aside.

Microwave on High for 1 minute:
> **¾ cup milk**

Pour milk into blender and add:
> **¼ cup sugar**
> **⅛ teaspoon salt**
> **12 ounces chocolate chips**
> **2 cups heavy cream**
> **1 teaspoon vanilla**
> **1 egg**
> **6 tablespoons rum (optional)**
> **2 ice cubes**

Blend until smooth.

Pour into small sherbet glasses. Garnish with:
> **whipped cream**
> **chocolate shavings**

Vanilla Custard Ice Cream

Preparation Time: 26 minutes   *8 servings*

Beat together in 4-cup glass measure:
2 cups milk
2 eggs
¾ cup sugar
Microwave on High for 5–6 minutes, stirring 2–3 times during that cooking time. Cool and blend in:
1 tablespoon vanilla
1 cup whipping cream
Pour into ice cream freezer and process.

Chocolate Custard Ice Cream

Preparation Time: 30 minutes   *8 servings*

Combine in 2-quart glass measure:
½ cup sugar
2 tablespoons flour
¼ teaspoon salt
Beat in:
2 cups milk
2 eggs
Microwave uncovered on High for 6–7 minutes or until mixture starts to thicken. Stir 2–3 times during that cooking time to prevent lumps. Then stir in until melted:
4 ounces sweet baking chocolate, broken into pieces
Cool.
Stir in:
2 cups heavy cream
1½ teaspoons vanilla
Add, if desired:
1 cup coconut, shredded
1 cup pecans, chopped
Process in ice cream freezer according to manufacturer's directions.

Individual Cheesecakes

Preparation Time: 15 minutes   Yields   24 cakes

Microwave on High for 1–2 minutes in glass mixing bowl until softened:
1 16-ounce package cream cheese
Beat until smooth, then blend in the following one at a time:
¾ cup sugar
2 eggs
1 tablespoon lemon juice
1 teaspoon vanilla
Microwave on High for 4–5 minutes, or until thickened. Stir occasionally.
Beat until smooth and set aside.
Line 24 muffin cups with paper liners and place in each:
1 vanilla wafer
Top each with:
reserved cream cheese filling
a dollop of preserves or jelly
Refrigerate or freeze.

Bread Pudding

Preparation Time: 15 minutes   8 servings

Place in 9-inch round baking dish:
6 slices bread, cubed
Combine in 4-cup glass measure and microwave on High for 3 minutes:
2 cups milk
1 tablespoon butter
Stir in:
3 eggs, beaten
1 cup sugar
½ teaspoon cinnamon
¼ teaspoon salt
1 teaspoon vanilla
½ cup raisins
Pour over bread cubes. Microwave on High for 7–9 minutes.

Chocolate Bread Pudding

Preparation Time: 20 minutes   *8 servings*

Combine in glass loaf pan:
> **3 cups bread cumbs**
> **¼ cup sugar**
> **1 teaspoon cinnamon**
> **½ teaspoon nutmeg**
> **½ cup nuts, chopped**

Microwave on High for 2 minutes in 4-cup glass measure:
> **1½ cups milk**
> **2 squares semi-sweet chocolate**

Blend in:
> **½ cup sugar**
> **3 eggs**
> **1 teaspoon vanilla**

Pour over bread cubes. Microwave on High for 9–11 minutes.

CANDIES

Fun and Easy in the Microwave

• Candy is easy in the microwave—instead of stirring for hours, you stir only a few times to distribute the heat evenly.

• Coating Chocolate is ideal for beginners since it is predictably easy to work with. Check with candy-, craft-, or cake decorating supply houses in your area for the chocolate.

• Coating Chocolate simply needs to be melted and it is ready to use. "Real" chocolate, chocolate chips, and candy bars need to be tempered or mixed with other ingredients before they can be used for candy-making.

• Molds and a microwave candy thermometer, as well as paramount crystals, dry fondants, extracts, and desiccated coconut, are all available from candy-, craft-, or cake-decorating supply houses.

• Soft candies and cooked candies can be tackled successfully by beginners and experienced cooks alike, when using a microwave oven.

• Use a *microwave* candy thermometer. (The traditional cold water test can be used, but it is not as accurate as a thermometer.)

Candy stage	Temperature	Cold water test
Soft ball	235°–240°F	Forms a ball, but flattens when taken out of water
Firm ball	245°–250°F	Holds shape until pressed
Hard ball	255°–265°F	Holds its shape but is pliable
Soft crack	270°–290°F	Separates into threads
Hard crack	300°–310°F	Forms hard, brittle threads

• Use a glass measure with a handle. Candies are hot and round bowls are very difficult to handle. Measuring cups that are deep work better than shallow ones.

• Cover the glass measure with plastic wrap. The steam that is created dissolves the sugar that forms on the sides of the bowl. Be sure to stir the candy and scrape the sides of the bowl to keep all sugar dissolved.

• Avoid making candy on humid days. High altitude also affects the temperature. Check the temperature necessary to boil water in your home on the day you choose to make candy, then calculate the difference between that temperature and 212°F. Add or subtract that amount to the temperature(s) designated in the recipe you are using.

• Keep a constant check on the temperature of the candy while it is cooking. It may seem to take a long time until you notice a temperature change, but once it reaches 220°F it will rise quickly.

• Use a container large enough to handle the mixture. Boil-over often occurs with products containing milk and butter.

• When adding baking soda after microwaving, allow the mixture to stand for 2–3 minutes. The hot temperatures will not allow the baking soda to work to its full potential.

Easy Chocolate Chip Fudge

Preparation Time: 5 minutes   Yields 48 pieces

Combine in 8-cup glass bowl:
> **1 can sweetened condensed milk (see below)**
> **12 ounces chocolate chips**

Microwave on High for 1 to 1½ minutes or until chips melt when stirred (about 100°F).
Stir in:
> **½ cup nuts, chopped**
> **1 teaspoon vanilla**

Pour into buttered 8-inch square pan.

Sweetened Condensed Milk

Preparation Time: 5 minutes   Yields 14 ounces

Combine in 4-cup glass measure:
> **1½ cups sugar**
> **⅔ cup water**
> **½ cup butter**

Microwave on High for 1 minute. Stir. Microwave on High another minute. Stir. Microwave on High again for 1 minute and stir. Continue until mixture boils.
Combine in blender with:
> **2 cups dry milk**

Process until smooth.

Peanut Butter Fudge

Preparation Time: 5 minutes   Yields 48 pieces

Combine in 8-cup glass bowl:
> **1 can sweetened condensed milk (see above)**
> **12 ounces peanut butter chips**

Microwave on High for 1 to 1½ minutes or until chips melt when stirred (about 100°F).
Stir in:
> **½ cup peanuts, chopped**
> **1 teaspoon vanilla**

Pour into buttered 8-inch square pan.

Butterscotch Fudge

Preparation Time: 5 minutes   *Yields 48 pieces*

Combine in 8-cup glass bowl:
> **1 can sweetened condensed milk (see page 181)**
> **12 ounces butterscotch chips**

Microwave on High for 1 to 1½ minutes or until chips melt when stirred (about 100°F).

Stir in:
> **1 teaspoon vanilla**

Pour into buttered 8-inch square pan.

Vanilla Fudge

Preparation Time: 5 minutes   *Yields 48 pieces*

Combine in 8-cup glass bowl:
> **1 can sweetened condensed milk (see page 181)**
> **12 ounces white chocolate chips (available at supply stores)**

Microwave on High for 1 to 1½ minutes or until chips melt when stirred (about 100°F).

Stir in:
> **½ cup nuts, chopped**
> **1 teaspoon vanilla**

Pour into buttered 8-inch square pan.

Special Fudge Sauce

Preparation Time: 8 minutes   *Yields   2½ cups*

Combine and microwave on High for 6–7 minutes until bubbly:
> **2 cups brown sugar**
> **⅔ cup corn syrup**
> **⅓ cup cocoa**
> **½ cup light cream**

Stir in:
> **1 teaspoon vanilla**

Serve warm over ice cream.

Melting Coatings

Place in 4-cup glass measure:
1 pound coating wafers or pieces
Microwave on High for 2 minutes. Stir. Microwave on High another
minute. Stir. Microwave on High in 30 second intervals until chocolate is
smooth when stirred.
Note: Be sure to stir. Chocolate may retain its shape but still be melted. Do
not overcook; the chocolate can be ruined.

Dipping Chocolates

To dip chocolates, melt the coating as directed above. Prepare your favorite centers and dip them into coatings.
Dried fruits work well (If you use fresh fruits, be sure they are clean and
dry before dipping.): **strawberries, apple slices, apricots, raisins, pineapple chunks, banana slices.**

Try dry finger foods: **sugar wafers, round crackers sandwiched with
peanut butter, pretzels, potato chips, animal crackers, any cookies,
nuts.**

Molded Candies

To mold candies, pour melted coating chocolated into molds. Tap molds
until all the air bubbles come to the top and then burst. Chill until candies
fall out of the molds when tapped gently. The time will vary with the
mold (larger molds take more time); for an average-sized mold, 10 to 15
minutes in the freezer should be enough. Unmold on a clean kitchen
towel to avoid breakage.

For ease in filling molds plastic squeeze bottles work well. Pour the
melted coating into a clean, dry, thin plastic squeeze bottle. Its lid may
need to be trimmed to allow the coating to flow easily. Squeeze until each
mold is full. When the bottle is empty, place it in the freezer for a few
minutes, then squeeze and shake out the hardened coating. These chips
can be added to the next batch or eaten!

Clusters and Barks

Clusters are made by adding dry ingredients to melted coating chocolate which is then spooned onto waxed paper and cooled until set.
Barks are made by adding dry ingredients to melted coating chocolate which is then spread onto waxed paper and cooled until set. These are then broken into pieces.
Barks and clusters are usually made with dry ingredients of small pieces: nuts, raisins, coconut, broken pretzels, chinese noodles, cereals and anything else you would like covered with chocolate.

Rocky Road

Preparation Time: 15 minutes

Combine in 2-quart glass measure:
> **1 pound milk chocolate coating**
> **1 cup peanut butter**

Microwave on High for 3–5 minutes, or until soft.
Stir until smooth. Stir into chocolate to coat:
> **1 pound miniature marshmallows**
> **1 pound salted peanuts**

Spread on waxed paper or drop by spoonfuls onto waxed paper. Allow to set.

Tiger Butter

Preparation Time: 15 minutes

Microwave on High for 2 minutes:
2 pounds white coating chocolate
4 tablespoons paramount crystals
1 cup peanut butter

Stir. Microwave on High for 2 more minutes. Stir. Microwave on High for another minute, or until mixture is smooth when stirred.

Spread on a waxed paper-lined cookie sheet and top with:
1 cup melted milk chocolate

Marble by swirling scraper through the mixture. Cut into squares when set.

Zebra Butter

Preparation Time: 15 minutes

Microwave on High for 2 minutes:
2 pounds white coating chocolate
4 tablespoons paramount crystals
1 cup desiccated coconut (dried)

Stir. Microwave on High for 2 more minutes. Stir. Microwave on High another minute, or until mixture is smooth when stirred.

Spread on a waxed paper-lined cookie sheet and top with:
1 cup melted dark chocolate

Marble by swirling scraper through the mixture. Cut into squares when set.

Chocolate Swirl

Preparation Time: 15 minutes

Microwave on High for 2 minutes:
2 pounds milk chocolate coating wafers
4 tablespoons paramount crystals

Stir. Microwave on High for 2 more minutes. Stir. Microwave on High another minute, or until mixture is smooth when stirred.

Spread on a waxed paper-lined cookie sheet and top with:
1 cup melted dark chocolate

Marble by swirling scraper through the mixture. Cut into squares when set.

Mint Swirl

Preparation Time: 15 minutes

Microwave on High for 2 minutes:
> **2 pounds green coating wafers**
> **4 tablespoons paramount crystals**

Stir. Microwave on High for 2 more minutes. Stir. Microwave on High another minute, or until mixture is smooth when stirred.
Stir in:
> **6–8 drops peppermint oil**

Spread on a waxed paper-lined cookie sheet and top with:
> **1 cup melted chocolate**

Marble by swirling scraper through the mixture. Cut into squares when set.

Note: Oils are available through candy supply houses or most pharmacies. Do not use extracts which will ruin your coating.

Layered Mints

Preparation Time: 15 minutes

Microwave on High for 2 minutes.
> **2 pounds dark chocolate coating wafers**
> **4 tablespoons paramount crystals**

Stir. Microwave on High for 2 more minutes. Stir. Microwave on High another minute, or until mixture is smooth when stirred.
Spread on a waxed paper-lined cookie sheet. Allow to set and top with:
> **1 cup melted dark chocolate**

Then follow the instructions for Mint Swirl (above), spreading the mixture on top of the melted dark chocolate. Do NOT marble. Repeat Mint Swirl directions again, adding another layer to the already prepared layers. Do NOT marble. Cut into squares when set.

Silky Way

Combine in glass measuring cup:
> **1 cup marshmallow creme (7 ounce jar)**
> **½ cup melted dark coating chocolate (see Melting Coatings, page 183)**

Allow to set and cut into squares. Dip in melted milk chocolate.

Easy Cream Centers for Dipping or Eating

Preparation Time: 5 minutes

Microwave on High for 1 minute:
> **1 pound butter**
> **¾ cup heavy cream**

Stir in:
> **1 pound dry fondant**

Knead by hand until smooth and creamy.

Note: This is a basic mixture and can be used as above or colored and flavored as desired:
> **Chocolate—knead in melted chocolate squares**
> **Mint—add a few drops peppermint and a few drops of red or green food coloring**
> **Nut—knead in finely chopped nuts**
> **Fruit and nut—knead in candied fruit and ground nuts**

Try your own concoctions. The texture and consistency of this mixture can be altered by the amount of fondant used.

Moist Coconut Centers

Microwave on High for 1 minute, or until boiling:
> **1 cup light corn syrup**

Stir in:
> **½ pound dessicated coconut (dry)**
> **½ teaspoon coconut extract**

Peanut Butter Centers

Combine in mixer bowl:
> **2 cups peanut butter**
> **¼ cup margarine or butter**
> **1 pound powdered sugar**
> **1 teaspoon vanilla**

Shape into balls and dip in melted milk chocolate coating (see Melting Coatings, page 183).

Caramel Krispies

Combine in mixing bowl:
> **½ pound caramel, melted**
> **1½ cups crisp rice cereal**

Pack into greased 8-inch square pan. Allow to set and cut into squares. Dip in melted milk chocolate coating (see Melting Coatings, page 183).

Turtles

Arrange nuts in clusters on buttered wax paper:
> **¼ pound pecans, cashews, or almonds**

Top each cluster with:
> **dab of melted chocolate coating (see Melting Coatings, page 183)**

Top each cluster with:
> **caramel, about ¼ pound in all**

Top each cluster with:
> **melted coating of your choice, being sure to cover caramel**

Jellies

Preparation Time: 1 hour   *Yields 60 pieces*

Microwave on High for 3 minutes in 4-cup glass measure:
> **1 cup water**

Stir in:
> **6-ounce package flavored gelatin**
> **2 envelopes unflavored gelatin**
> **1 cup cold water**

Stir until dissolved. Pour into greased 9 × 13 baking pan. Chill until firm. Cut into squares. Eat as is or dip in chocolate coating (see Melting Coatings, page 183).

Nutty Bars

Preparation Time: 30 minutes   Yields   60 pieces

Microwave in 2-quart glass measure for 4 minutes:
> **4 cups quick rolled oats**
> **½ cup margarine**

Stir in and microwave on High for 2 minutes:
> **1 cup brown sugar**
> **½ cup corn syrup**

Pour into greased 9 × 13 baking pan. Top with the following chocolate mixture:

Combine in 2-cup measure and microwave on High for 1 minute, or until melted:
> **⅔ cup chocolate chips**
> **¼ cup peanut butter**

Allow to set and cut into squares.

Crispy Bars

Preparation Time: 30 minutes   Yields 48 bars

Combine in 3-quart glass casserole and microwave on High for 3 minutes:
> **¼ cup margarine or butter**
> **5 cups mini-marshmallows or 40 large marshmallows**

Stir until smooth and then stir in:
> **5 cups crisp rice cereal**

Press mixture into buttered 9 × 13 baking pan. Chill and cut into squares.

Peanut Crispy Bars

Preparation Time: 30 Minutes   Yields   48 bars

Combine in 3-quart glass casserole and microwave on High for 3 minutes:
> **¼ cup margarine or butter**
> **5 cups mini-marshmallows or 40 large marshmallows**
> **⅓ cup peanut butter**

Stir until smooth and then stir in:
> **5 cups crisp rice cereal**
> **1 cup peanuts**

Press mixture into buttered 9 × 13 baking pan. Chill and cut into squares.
Dip each in milk chocolate coating (see Melting Coatings, page 183).

Truffles

Preparation Time: 1½ hours

Combine in 2-quart glass measure:
> **1 cup heavy cream**
> **1 pound plus 6 ounces semi-sweet chocolate, chopped**

Microwave on High for 2 minutes. Stir until smooth. Cool. Drop by tea-spoonfuls onto waxed paper. Refrigerate 1 hour. Roll into balls. Dip in coating chocolate or roll in nuts (see Melting Coatings, page 183).

Cordial Truffles

Preparation Time: 1½ hours

Combine in 2-quart glass measure:
> **1 cup heavy cream**
> **1 pound plus 6 ounces semi-sweet chocolate, chopped**
> **3 tablespoons kirshwasser, rum, or cherry juice**

Microwave on High for 2 minutes. Stir until smooth. Cool. Drop by tea-spoonfuls onto waxed paper. Refrigerate 1 hour. Roll into balls. Dip in coating chocolate (see Melting Coatings, page 183) or roll in nuts.

Cherry Cordials

Preparation Time: 30 minutes   Yields   24 pieces

Drain and then soak in kirshwasser or brandy, if desired, overnight:
> **1 jar maraschino cherries**

Combine and microwave on High for 30 seconds:
> **½ cup dry fondant**
> **3 tablespoons maraschino cherry juice, from soaked cherries**

Line cordial molds with melted dark coating chocolate (see Melting Coatings, page 183). Dot with cherry juice mixture. Add to each mold maraschino cherries, drained and dried. Seal with melted dark chocolate coating.

Peanut Brittle

Preparation Time: 20 minutes

Combine in 2-quart glass measure and microwave on High for 5 minutes:

1½ cups sugar
½ cup light corn syrup
½ cup water
dash salt

Stir and then microwave on High for 13–15 minutes or to 300°F. Allow to stand 2 minutes and then stir in:

2 cups peanuts
1 tablespoon butter
1 teaspoon baking soda
1 teaspoon vanilla

Pour onto buttered cookie sheet. Cool and break into pieces.

Almond Butter Crunch

Preparation Time: 12 minutes

Combine in 2-quart glass measure and microwave on High for 12 minutes or to 300°F:

1 cup butter
1⅓ cups granulated sugar
1 tablespoon corn syrup
3 tablespoons water

Stir in:

1 cup almonds, chopped

Pour onto buttered cookie sheet. Cool and break into pieces.

Peanutbutter Fingers

Preparation time: 15 minutes

Combine in 2-quart glass measure and microwave on High to 310°F:

1 cup granulated sugar
⅓ cup corn syrup
⅓ cup water

Stir in:

1 cup peanut butter

Spread to desired thickness on buttered cookie sheet. Score with knife or pastry wheel. Break apart when cool.

Toffee

Preparation Time: 10 minutes

Combine in 2-quart glass measure and microwave on High for 4 minutes:

> **1 cup butter**
> **1⅓ cups sugar**
> **1 tablespoon light corn syrup**
> **2 tablespoons water**

Stir. Microwave on High for 6–8 minutes or to 300°F. Stir in:

> **1 teaspoon vanilla**
> **⅓ cup nuts, finely chopped**

Pour onto buttered cookie sheet and score with knife or pastry wheel. Top with:

> **½ cup chocolate pieces, melted**
> **¼ cup nuts, finely chopped**

Chill and break into pieces.

Caramel Corn

Preparation Time: 7 minutes

Combine in 2-quart glass measure and microwave on High for 3 minutes, or to boiling:

> **1 cup brown sugar**
> **½ cup butter**
> **¼ cup light corn syrup**
> **½ teaspoon salt**

Microwave at 30% for 4 minutes. Let stand 2 minutes and stir in:

> **½ teaspoon baking soda**
> **⅔ cup nuts, chopped**

Pour over:

> **4 quarts popped popcorn (16 cups)**

Mix until popcorn is coated and nuts are well distributed.

Caramels

Preparation Time: 20 minutes

Combine in 2-quart glass measure and microwave on High for 8 minutes, or until boiling:

1 cup granulated sugar
1 cup dark corn syrup
1 cup heavy cream
¼ cup butter

Stir well and microwave on High for 10 more minutes or until temperature reaches 250°F. Stir often. Pour into buttered 11 × 7 baking pan. Chill and cut into squares.

Note: 1 cup chopped nuts can be stirred in before pouring mixture into buttered pan.

Big Batch Caramels

Preparation Time: 1 hour

Microwave in 4-quart bowl on High for 1 minute:

1 cup butter

Stir in:

2 cups sugar
2 cups light corn syrup
1 cup heavy cream

Microwave on High for 24 minutes. Stir in:

1 cup heavy cream

Insert candy thermometer and cook to 245°F. Stir in:

1 tablespoon vanilla

Pour into buttered 9 × 13 pan. Cool. Cut into squares.

Sponge Candy

Preparation Time: 10 minutes

Combine in 2-quart glass measure and microwave on High for 8–10 minutes or until temperature reaches 300°F:

1 cup granulated sugar
1 cup light corn syrup

Allow to stand 2 minutes. Stir in:

4 teaspoons baking soda
1 teaspoon maple flavoring

Spread onto buttered baking sheet. Chill and break into pieces, which may be dipped in chocolate (see Melting Coatings, page 183).

Hard Candies

Preparation Time: 6 minutes

Combine in 2-quart glass measure and microwave on High for 6 minutes, or until mixture comes to a full boil:

2 cups granulated sugar
⅓ cup water
½ cup corn syrup

Stir well and continue to microwave on High for 8 minutes or until temperature reaches 300°F. Pour into buttered hard candy molds or onto buttered cookie sheet. Score with sharp knife or pastry wheel. Chill and break apart.

APPETIZERS AND BEVERAGES

Bacon Appetizer

Arrange **1 pound bacon,** cut in half lengthwise, on paper towel. Place paper towel on meat rack or paper plate. Cover with another paper towel. Microwave on High for 4–5 minutes. Assemble favorite fillings:

> **water chestnuts**
> **pineapple chunks**
> **pretzel nuggets**
> **chicken nuggets**
> **fish nuggets**
> **vegetable nuggets**
> **hot dog chunks**
> **liverwurst**
> **cheese chunks**
> **bread**
> **chicken livers, cut in pieces**
> **apple chunks**
> **mushrooms**
> **shrimp**
> **lobster**
> **olives**

Wrap bacon around filling. Secure with wooden picks. Place on fresh paper towel, either on the rack or on a paper plate. Cover with another paper towel. Microwave on High for 6–7 minutes or until bacon is crisp.

Butterflied Wieners

Preparation Time: 6 minutes   *8 servings*

Prepare:
> **1 pound jumbo hot dogs**

by cutting each wiener crosswise into 3 pieces. Then cut each piece in half lengthwise to make 6 pieces. Slit each piece through its ends leaving a ¼-inch join in center. Set aside.
Mix in 1½-quart casserole:
> **¼ cup honey**
> **1 bottle barbecue sauce**

Cover and microwave on High for 1 minute. Stir. Add hot dogs. Microwave on High for 3 minutes or until ends curl. Serve with toothpicks.

Spicy Stuffed Mushrooms

Preparation Time: 20 minutes   Yields 20–24 mushrooms

Microwave on High for 4 minutes:

1 pound italian sausage

Stir in:

2 tablespoons catsup
⅛ teaspoon oregano
dash garlic powder

Microwave on High for 1 minute.
Fill:

20–24 mushroom caps

Top with:

mozzarella cheese, grated
fresh parsley

Microwave on High for 2–3 minutes until caps are warm and cheese is melted.

Ham Roll-Ups

Preparation Time: 5 minutes

Layer:

cooked ham slices
swiss cheese slices

Top with:

cranberry-orange relish

Roll and slice each roll into 4 pieces. Secure with toothpicks. Microwave at 80% until cheese begins to melt. Serve warm.

Light Vegetable Dip

Preparation Time: 15 minutes   Yields   2½ cups

Pierce and microwave on High for 6–7 minutes:

1 eggplant (about 1 pound)

Set aside to cool.

Combine in small bowl:

1 small onion, minced
½ pepper, minced
1 clove garlic, minced
1 teaspoon lemon juice
½ teaspoon salt
⅛ teaspoon pepper

Microwave on High for 2 minutes or until vegetables are limp. Place vegetable mixture in blender with:

1 cup plain yogurt

Add pulp scooped from eggplant and blend until mixed well. Cover and chill thoroughly. Serve with antipasto.

Light Fruit Salad

Preparation Time: 20 minutes   4 servings

Drain **juice** from 8-ounce can unsweetened pineapple chunks into 2-cup glass measure and mix with the following ingredients until smooth:

1 tablespoon lemon juice
1 egg, beaten
1½ teaspoons cornstarch

Microwave on High for 3 minutes or until mixture thickens and boils, stirring twice during cooking time. Chill about 15 minutes, then mix in:

⅓ cup plain yogurt

Pour over:

1 apple, cut into chunks
1 banana, sliced
1 orange, sectioned and cut
pineapple chunks

Cream Cheese Fruit Spread

Preparation Time: 2 minutes   **Yields 1 cup**

Place in 1-quart glass bowl:

1 package (8 ounces) cream cheese

Microwave uncovered on High for 45–60 seconds or until **softened.**
Stir in:

¼–½ cup dried fruit and raisin mixture, diced
2 tablespoons brown sugar
¼ teaspoon cinnamon

If desired, add 2 tablespoons chopped nuts with fruit. Store leftover
spread in refrigerator. For ease in spreading, microwave on **High for 30–60**
seconds, stirring once.

Boiling Water in a Cup

Microwave on High for 2½–3 minutes:

1 cup water in 10-ounce mug

Microwave on High for 4½–5½ minutes:

1 cup water in each of 2 10-ounce mugs

When water boils, stir in instant hot drink mix or soup.

Spiced Cider

Preparation Time: 8 minutes   **Yields   1 quart**

Mix in microwave-safe 2-quart container:

1 quart apple cider
¼ cup light brown sugar
½ teaspoon whole cloves
½ teaspoon whole allspice
1 cinnamon stick
dash of salt

Microwave on High for 6 minutes

Hot Chocolate from Scratch

Preparation Time: 8 minutes   *2 servings*

Blend together in small bowl:

> **2 tablespoons unsweetened cocoa powder**
> **2 tablespoons sugar**
> **2 tablespoons hot water**

Cover and microwave on High for 1 minute.

Stir in:

> **1¾ cups milk**

Cover and microwave on High for 3½–4½ minutes, stiring 3 times during that cooking time.

Stir in:

> **¼ teaspoon vanilla**

Dip mixture into 2 10-ounce microwave-safe mugs. Top each with a **marshmallow,** if desired, then microwave on High for 1 minute.

The
Menu Planning
Guide

Menu Planning and Meal Preparation Using Your Microwave

Microwave ovens enhance the wishes and simplify the tasks of all good cooks!

Taste and nutrition, appearance, color, and texture can all be successfully achieved in a microwave. What's more, food preparation is less time- and energy-consuming!

It is possible—and easy—to prepare full meals in a microwave oven. Planning is necessary, as it is when using a conventional stove and oven. The payoff is nutritional, tasty food, prepared with minimal effort and time.

Making Meals in a Microwave

There are several ways to maximize your microwave's capacity in meal preparation. Here are particular methods that work well:

• Prepare *meals* ahead of time so they can be microwaved in minutes at mealtime. Then organize those meals in your refrigerator or freezer so that their cooking times correspond to the time intervals you have available. A blue label could indicate a 4-minute preparation; a white label an 8-minute preparation; a red label a 12-minute preparation, and so on.

• Fix *casseroles* when you have time, then freeze them so they're available for reheating when you're short on time.

   1. Although large-quantity casseroles may require nearly as much time in a microwave as in a conventional oven, there are certain advantages to using a microwave in their preparation. As with other foods, nutrients are better retained. In addition, preparation and cleanup are quick and easy because of using one dish for all steps.
   2. Although precooking of certain elements may be necessary, some of that can be done with considerable time-saving in the microwave. For example, chopped onions or peppers can be precooked quickly in the same dish in which the casserole will be cooked and served.

3. In some cases, pasta or rice need not be precooked (see Lasagna recipe, page 83); it can be included in its dehydrated form. If the recipe calls for pasta or rice to be cooked, you may save that step by adding extra liquid (2 tablespoons per ounce) and by cooking the casserole longer (add 1 minute per 2 ounces of dehydrated pasta or rice).

4. Leftovers can be frozen and reheated in single or multiple portion sizes. Because of the cooking method, these extras don't have a "left-over" taste and they remain moist and flavorful when properly covered and reheated.

• Program your microwave so your meal is prepared when you expect to arrive home.

• Plan a meal with various dishes, microwaving according to each food's cooking and standing times.

1. Foods that take longer to cook usually have a longer standing time. Cook those foods first because they will also hold their heat a proportionately longer time.

Foods that have a high content of water, sugar, or fat usually hold their cooking temperatures well.

2. Foods with shorter cooking times should be cooked last because they can be cooked during the other food's standing time.

3. Foods with similar cooking times can usually be cooked at the same time if their cooking times are added together.

4. A sample meal—

Microwave a 3-pound chicken for 20 minutes. Remove from oven. Let stand 10–12 minutes.

Next, microwave 4 baked potatoes for 12 minutes. Remove from oven. Let stand 4–5 minutes.

Finally, microwave 10-ounce pack of vegetables for 4 minutes.

Serve chicken, potatoes, and vegetables with tossed salad and rolls, and cherry crunch (prepared earlier) for dessert.

• Do Meal-in-One cooking. It is possible, if your oven is large enough, to cook several dishes at a time in your microwave. To determine whether this method is a good one for the menu you have chosen, consider these basic guidelines:

1. If all the foods you are preparing take less than 15 minutes each, add their cooking times together and microwave all at once.

2. If all the foods require between 15 and 35 minutes each, add their cooking times together, then subtract 5 minutes to arrive at the right length of cooking for doing all foods in the oven at once.

3. If any one food takes more than 35 minutes, all other foods can be cooked during that one food's cooking time. (Add or remove dishes as needed while cooking.)

If you prepare more than one dish at a time in your microwave, remember this:

1. Use the oven's rack only when there is not enough room for all the dishes on the floor of the oven. Remove the rack if it is not needed.

2. Since foods on the rack receive and absorb the microwaves first, place foods there that require longer cooking time. For example, spare ribs and potatoes would be set on the rack, while the corn would be placed on the floor of the oven. Or pork chops and potatoes would be positioned on the rack and boxed vegetables on the bottom of the oven.

3. If all foods can be placed in the oven at once and have similar cooking times, reverse the dishes halfway through the cooking, moving those on the rack to the floor and those on the bottom to the rack.

4. When possible, stagger the dishes, so that those on the rack are not directly above those on the oven floor.

5. Use High whenever you cook more than one food at a time.

6. Browning dishes and crispers cannot be used when more than one item is being cooked or when the rack is being used.

7. Foods that cook very quickly, such as breads that are being reheated, should be done separately.

Menu Suggestions and Procedures for Meals in the Microwave

Meat Loaf
Scalloped Potatoes
Vegetable
Chocolate Pudding

Preparation Time: 25 minutes   *4 servings*

---

1. Prepare chocolate pudding (page 170) in advance and refrigerate.
2. Prepare meat loaf (page 81) in loaf pan.
3. Prepare scalloped potatoes (page 54) in another loaf pan.
4. Unwrap 10-ounce package of frozen vegetables and place in serving dish.
5. Insert shelf in oven. Place meat loaf and potatoes on shelf and vegetable on the floor of the oven.
6. Microwave on High for 20–25 minutes or until meat loaf reaches 135°F.

Beef Roast
Roasted Potatoes
Carrots
Salad
Fresh Mixed Fruit and Brownies

Preparation Time: 50 minutes   *6–8 servings*

---

1. Prepare brownies (pages 151–159) several hours in advance and set aside.
2. Follow instructions for chuck roast (page 78) by combining roast, potatoes, and carrots in a cooking bag with juice, seasoning, and thickening.
3. While dinner is cooking set table, prepare salad and mixed fruit.

Pork Chops
Baked Potatoes
Vegetable
Salad
Tapioca Pudding

Preparation Time: 30 minutes   *4 servings*

1. Prepare tapioca pudding (page 172) several hours in advance and refrigerate.
3. Place 4 pork chops that weigh about ½ pound each in a glass baking dish. Cover with plastic wrap or place in cooking bag.
3. Scrub and pierce 4 medium-sized baking potatoes.
4. Unwrap 10-ounce package of a frozen vegetable and place in serving dish.
5. Insert shelf in oven. Place pork chops and potatoes on shelf and vegetable on the floor of the oven.
6. Microwave for 20–25 minutes at 70% or until pork chops reach 170°F.

Note: Meats with similar weights or cooking times can be substituted for the pork chops; for instance, two pounds of spare ribs or chicken can be used.

Chicken
Stuffing
Mixed Vegetable
Salad
Quick Cherry Crunch

1. Prepare Quick Cherry Crunch (page 169) several hours in advance and set aside.
2. Prepare favorite stuffing in shallow baking pan.
3. Arrange prepared chicken pieces on top of stuffing.
4. Unwrap 10-ounce package frozen mixed vegetables.
5. Place chicken and stuffing on shelf in microwave and place mixed vegetables on the floor of the oven.
6. Microwave for suggested cooking time for chicken (see pages 100–105).
7. Set table, prepare salad and dessert.

Chicken
Rice
Vegetable
Salad
Cupcakes

Preparation Time: 25 minutes   *4 servings*

1. Place 2 pounds of chicken pieces on microwave-safe baking dish. Sprinkle with browning powder or paprika. Cover with plastic wrap or place in cooking bag.
2. Combine 1 cup rice, 2 cups water, 1 tablespoon butter, and 1 teaspoon salt in large covered casserole.
3. Unwrap 10-ounce package of frozen vegetable and place in serving dish.
4. Insert shelf in oven. Place chicken and rice on shelf and vegetable on the floor of the oven.
5. Microwave on High for 20–25 minutes or until rice is tender and chicken comes away from the bones.
6. Set table, prepare salad, and mix cupcakes. Bake just as you serve the main course.

Chicken Cordon Bleu
Potato Stuffing
Green Bean Bake
Cole Slaw
Chocolate Mousse

Preparation Time: 50–60 minutes   *6–8 servings*

1. Prepare cole slaw and mousse (page 175). (These are best if prepared a few hours ahead of serving time.)
2. Prepare potato stuffing (page 55) in shallow baking pan.
3. Arrange prepared chicken pieces (page 101) on top of stuffing.
4. Prepare green bean bake (page 51).
5. Place chicken and stuffing on shelf in microwave and place green bean casserole on the floor of the oven.
6. Microwave on High for 10 minutes, reversing the positions of the two casseroles halfway through the cooking time.

Note: This is an ideal meal to serve to guests because it can all be prepared ahead of time, heated at meal time, then served right from the oven without much last-minute preparation.

Fish
Mashed Potatoes
Stewed Tomatoes
Salad
Lemon Chiffon Pie

---

1. Prepare lemon chiffon pie (page 165) several hours in advance and refrigerate.
2. Prepare mashed potatoes (page 54). Cover and set aside.
3. Prepare stewed tomatoes. Cover and set aside.
4. Arrange fish in baking dish and prepare as desired (see pages 114–117).
5. Place fish on shelf in microwave and place potatoes and tomatoes on the floor of the oven to reheat as the fish cooks.
6. Microwave for suggested cooking time for fish.
7. Set table and prepare salad and beverage.

Breaded Fish Fillets
Twice-Baked Potatoes
Green Bean Bake
Peach Crumb Pie

---

1. Bake pie shell (page 163).
2. Prepare pie filling and bake (page 163).
3. Bake potatoes (page 48) and set aside.
4. Cook beans (page 51) and set aside.
5. Prepare potatoes for second baking.
6. Finish bean casserole in oven, cover, and set aside.
7. Preheat browning dish and cook fish fillets. Set aside.
8. Finish potatoes.

Spaghetti
Meat Sauce
Tossed Salad
Garlic Bread
Ice Cream

Preparation Time: 25 minutes   *6–8 servings*

1. Prepare ice cream (page 176).
2. Partially cook noodles (see page 69).
3. Prepare tossed salad and garlic bread while noodles cook. Prepare garlic bread by slicing a loaf of Italian bread and spreading it with garlic butter made by blending ¼ pound butter with 1 clove garlic. Wrap loaf in napkin and set aside.
4. Prepare sauce (page 88) or heat a jar of your favorite spaghetti sauce by placing probe in the jar and heating to 130°F. Pour sauce over noodles and toss gently. Return to oven and microwave on High for 6 more minutes. Top with parmesan cheese.
5. Microwave garlic bread on High for 1 minute.

Note: Spaghetti squash can be substituted for the noodles.

Bacon and Cheese Omelet
Cinnamon Rolls
Frozen Orange Drink

1. Saute bacon in microwave (page 92).
2. Prepare carmel nut sticky buns (page 135) or heat frozen cinnamon rolls. Cover and set aside.
3. Prepare omelet (page 36).
4. While omelet cooks, prepare frozen orange drink by combining the following in a blender:

> **2 cups milk**
> **1 6-ounce can frozen concentrated orange juice (page 215)**
> **1 egg**
> **1 tablespoon sugar**
> **1 teaspoon vanilla**
> **6 ice cubes, partially crushed**

Stuffed Hot Dogs
Cream of Broccoli Soup
Apple Crisp

1. Prepare apple crisp (page 168) several hours in advance and set aside.
2. Microwave bacon for half the normal cooking time (see page 92).
3. Prepare white sauce (page 27).
4. Stuff and wrap hot dogs with cheese and bacon.
5. Add broccoli to white sauce and finish soup (page 63).
6. Cook hot dogs (page 98).
7. Serve hot dogs in rolls with soup.

Tips

- To soften ½ pound butter or cream cheese, microwave in a glass dish on High for 30–45 seconds.
- To melt 2 tablespoons butter or margarine, microwave in a glass dish on High for 30 seconds.
- For crisp bread crumbs, microwave 1 cup in 2 tablespoons melted butter on High for 1 minute.
- Crisp stale chips or crackers by microwaving between paper towels on High for 20–30 seconds.
- Soften hard brown sugar by placing it in a glass dish with a wedge of apple or slice of bread. Microwave on High for 30 seconds per cup.
- To toast nuts, spread in single layer and microwave on High for 3 minutes per cup, stirring every minute.
- To melt 8 ounces of chocolate, microwave on High for 1 minute. Stir, then repeat procedure at 30-second intervals until chocolate is melted. Always be sure to stir before adding more time.
- Microwave tomatoes on High for 30 seconds for easy peeling.
- Microwave frozen concentrate in paper or plastic containers on High for 30 seconds to make mixing easier.
- Soften ice cream to custardy consistency by microwaving on High for 10–15 seconds.
- Separate slices of frozen bacon easily by microwaving them on High for 15 seconds.
- Reheat leftover pancakes, waffles, and sweet rolls for a quick, just-baked taste. Wrap in paper towel and microwave on High for 8–10 seconds.
- Soften tortillas between paper towels. For 12 tortillas microwave on High for 1 minute.
- Reheat leftover coffee for just-perked flavor. Microwave on High for 2 minutes per cup.
- Instead of preparing a hot water bottle, microwave a wet wash cloth in a heavy plastic bag for 30 seconds.
- Use a temperature probe when liquids are to be at an exact temperature.
- Clean your oven by first microwaving a soapy dishcloth on High for 30 seconds. Then wipe the oven with the clean cloth.

Index